MW00696580

The Path to a Woman's Happiness

Other Books by Cindy Schaap

A Meek and Quiet Spirit
Lessons for Wives and Mothers
from Women in the New Testament

A Wife's Purpose

Bright Side Planner/Journal

From the Coal Mines to the Gold Mines
An Authorized Biography of Russell Anderson

Living on the Bright Side
Principles for Lasting Joy, Especially for Ladies

Silk and Purple
Lessons for Wives and Mothers
from Women in the Old Testament

The Fundamental Man
An Authorized Biography of Jack Frasure Hyles

Training Kings and Queens

The
ℙ𝒜TH
to a Woman's
HAPPINESS

Cindy Schaap

© 2007
CHRISTIAN WOMANHOOD
8400 Burr Street
Crown Point, Indiana 46307
www.christianwomanhood.org
(219) 365-3202

ISBN: 0-9793892-4-0

Credits:
Cover and Unit Photographs:
Courtesy of Pastor Jack Schaap
Layout and Design: Mrs. Linda Stubblefield
Proofreaders: Mrs. Rena Fish, Mrs. Jane Grafton

All Scripture references used in this book
are from the King James Bible.

Printed and Bound in the United States

Dedication

*T*HIS BOOK IS DEDICATED to my aunt, Earlyne Stephens. Though she has known her share of heartaches, at the age of 88, she is still one of the most positive people I know. Her sweet spirit causes her to see the good in everyone and to speak only that good. She represents all of the women I have been blessed to know who have taught me about the true happiness which comes only from Jesus Christ.

Acknowledgments

I WOULD LIKE TO THANK my husband, Dr. Jack Schaap, for being a great husband, as well as a great pastor and teacher, and for helping lead me down the path to happiness.

I appreciate Mrs. Rena Fish and Mrs. Jane Grafton for their help in proofreading this manuscript. Rena, your expert proofing and editing has been invaluable to Christian Womanhood publications since 1998, and I am grateful. Jane, your work as managing editor of the publications I lead has been a blessing not only to the work, but also to me personally. You are a trusted worker and friend.

Linda Stubblefield has been the layout designer and typesetter of all eight of my books. She is the best in her craft and a tireless worker. It is a joy to work alongside you, Linda. Thanks for continually growing, not only in your work skills, but in every area of your life. I am a benefactor.

I love you all!

Table of Contents

Introduction

ECENTLY, I ASKED MY husband to describe what he liked about me. (This is probably one of those analytical questions that every husband dreads hearing.) My husband quickly responded by answering, "I like that you are a happy person."

It seems that every woman is seeking for happiness. This book, *The Path to a Woman's Happiness*, deals with lessons I have learned that have helped me to feel happy in life. In order to make this book more useful to you, I would like to begin by introducing you to some foundational principles for true happiness.

Happiness is best found when we realize that life was not given to us so that we could be happy. Life was given to us so that we might glorify our Creator and fulfill His purpose for our lives.

Happiness is best found when we who are married women realize that marriage was not given to us to make us happy. Marriage was given to us so that we might use it to glorify God and to win souls to Jesus Christ.

Happiness is best found when we who have husbands realize that our husbands were not given to us to make us feel happy and secure. Our husbands were given to us so that we might make them happy and encourage them.

Happiness is best found when we realize that relationships were not given to us to make us happy. They were given to us so that we might meet the needs of those involved.

A happy spirit is not given to us at all. We must, with God's help, create and protect our own happy spirit. Once that happy spirit is attained, we must realize that it is not ours to squander on selfish pleasures. A happy spirit is to be used to encourage others and, best of all, to encourage our God.

With these foundational principles in mind, I sincerely believe that the reading, understanding, and applying of this book's lessons will greatly enhance the happiness of your life, as they have mine. I am delighted that you are sharing this book with me.

Step 1

Be Aware
of God!

"God, Please Send Me a Hummingbird!"

A FEW YEARS AGO, THOUGH I had never seen a hummingbird at my house, I asked God to send one. I'm not even sure if I had a hummingbird feeder at the time, but I know that I knew almost nothing about attracting them. A few days later I saw a hummingbird flying amongst the flowers at the flower box by my dining room window. I was ecstatic!

"Lord," I prayed, "my family was not here to see the hummingbird. Could You send it again when my family is home?"

Sure enough, the following Sunday dinner, which was the only time that all four of us were for sure going to be together, the hummingbird arrived at the dining room window. I had not seen the hummingbird again until that time. "I love You too, Lord!" I said.

For the next couple of years, it still was quite rare for me to see a hummingbird. In August of 2001, our family took our first vacation since my husband had become pastor. It was also our last vacation before our oldest child got married. A hummingbird feeder located at the office of the condominium resort where we stayed in Colorado was loaded with hummingbirds. Because my husband and I are bird lovers, we went to a local drugstore, bought a hummingbird feeder and hummingbird food, and placed it on the deck of our condominium.

Every morning we read our Bible and prayed on the deck. Every morning we were distracted by dozens of hummingbirds coming to our feeder. My husband had a new camera, and he took 40 or 50 pictures of hummingbirds. (Our children came along on the trip, but they teased us about not taking nearly as many pictures of them as we did of the hummingbirds.) It was hard for us to say goodbye to "our" deck and to "our" hummingbirds.

I don't remember praying, but I do remember thinking to myself, "Wouldn't it be funny if I saw a hummingbird at our house when I got home?" It was August, and we had not seen a hummingbird at our house all summer.

We arrived home on a Saturday night. At 5:30 on Sunday morning, I got out of bed and saw a hummingbird flying around outside of our living room window. The hummingbird flew around in front of each window on our front porch for the entire day. All of the family saw it. After the day passed, the hummingbird left, and we never saw it again. It was as if a hummingbird had accidentally landed in our suitcase and then 24 hours later headed home again.

Since then, I have studied hummingbirds, and I saw a lot of hummingbird activity at our two feeders this year. God used a hummingbird to show me how much He likes to show off to those who will notice Him and give Him glory. Ever since that August 2001 vacation, every time I see a hummingbird, I say to God, "I know You love me, and I love You, too!"

A Thanksgiving Journal

NOVEMBER IS THE MONTH of my favorite holiday—Thanksgiving! On Thanksgiving Day, I take the time to read my journal from the past year. As many people know, I write down one thing God did each day to show me He loves me. I ask God to show Himself to me, and then I write down one way that He did. In order to celebrate Thanksgiving with you in this book, I am including three illustrations from my 2006 journal.

I had been corresponding with a reader named Shannon Truckner whose father was dying of cancer. Shortly after Shannon's father went to Heaven, she wrote me a letter telling me of his death. In that letter she shared that she had asked her father for something she should look for after he went to Heaven to remind her of him. He admonished her to look for goldfinches.

While reading Shannon's letter, I was interrupted by Gina Eyer, our customer service manager at Christian Womanhood. "Mrs. Schaap," she said, "the March 2006 issue of *Christian Womanhood* just arrived." She handed it to me, and as I looked at it, I was reminded that I had chosen a very beautiful picture of a goldfinch to be the cover for March. I looked at the magazine, and I looked at the letter from my friend Shannon, and I said as I so often do, "I see You, Jesus; I know You love me, and I love You too."

Knowing that Shannon receives the *Christian Womanhood* magazine each month, I knew she would be comforted by seeing its cover. I thanked God that He is interested in comforting Shannon, and I thanked Him that He leads and guides me as I make my daily decisions. We generally work two to three months ahead on our magazine, so I probably chose that goldfinch cover sometime in December or January. I had no way of knowing that it would be coming in the mail so soon after the death of Shannon's dad, nor did I know the significance of the goldfinch in his life. But God knew....

My Journal Entry—February 28, 2006...

I received a letter from a girl whose father just died. She asked him what to look for to think of him after he's gone. He said, "Goldfinches." Right after reading her letter, the March Christian Womanhood paper came in (which she gets), and a big goldfinch was on the front cover. God is so good! And so involved!!!!

———

I had a large picnic basket that I kept in my living room. I used it year round both for decoration and for storage. I noticed that it was becoming frayed at the edges. "I really don't feel like spending any money on a picnic basket," I said to myself. I enjoyed having a picnic basket in that place, and I needed it for storage, but I did not enjoy looking at its frayed edges. We try to keep our home liveable, but we also try to keep it first-class. Almost on a whim, I prayed, "God, send me a new picnic basket."

The following Sunday in church, a lady was visiting who teaches basket making. Her family introduced her as a visitor, and I believe it was an usher who shouted to Brother Schaap at the pulpit, "This lady has brought a picnic basket that she has made for Mrs. Schaap."

My husband, also on a whim (he doesn't usually do this type

of thing), said, "Well, bring the basket up to Mrs. Schaap right now."

I sit on the front row of the choir. This usher proceeded to walk down the aisle, up to the large platform, to my choir chair to hand me a beautiful, large, non-frayed picnic basket! It looked great for both storage and decoration. I was beaming! I almost felt like my face must have seemed a little overly excited about a picnic basket. I wanted to stand up and tell the whole church right then what God had done.

I couldn't believe the miraculous way that God had chosen to give me my basket. He had answered my prayer in *"great and mighty ways"* which I knew not and in a way that was *"exceeding abundantly above all"* that I could ask or think. I ask God to show Himself in ways that will seem great and miraculous to me, and He does!

On the handle of the picnic basket, the phrase "Basket of Blessings" was burned into the wood. I bowed my head during prayer and thanked the Lord, not only for showing Himself to me in such a unique way, but also for loving me and being interested in me. He even answers the prayers that are prayed on a whim.

My Journal Entry—May 7, 2006. . .

Great day at church. I received a picnic basket. I had prayed for a new one, a visitor brought one to church, and it was brought to me on the platform. God is good and answers my prayers in specific ways.

———

A young lady who had grown up in our church waited some time for God to give her a baby. A very healthy baby girl came along. It took some time for a second baby to come along, but finally one was on the way. Soon after, the doctor gave the devastating news that the baby "would look like a monster, would be terribly deformed, and would probably live at the most one year."

I was so proud of the reaction of this husband and wife as they carried the news in their hearts about the deformed baby, while the mother carried the baby in her womb.

Alyssa Riley

I cried and cried for this young mother. I also prayed. I wrote the young mother's name in my Bible beside Mark 10:27, which says, *"And Jesus looking upon them saith, With men it is impossible, but not with God: for with God all things are possible."* I read it frequently and prayed for her. A month or so later, the doctor told the young mother, "We believe there is a mistake; the baby might be normal." Just this past week, a completely healthy baby girl was born to this couple.

I know that God was answering the prayers of this dedicated mother and father. He was also answering their parents' and their pastor's prayers. But I also believe that God was answering mine. That is what keeps me praying. I see every answer to my prayers as a DIRECT answer from God to me.

My Journal Entry—July 22, 2006...

Emily Riley had a healthy baby girl today. Praise the Lord!

———

Allow me to summarize this chapter in the following five points.

1. Praise God for His willingness to answer our prayer for leadership and guidance. (Remember the goldfinch.)
2. Praise God for His interest in showing Himself to us through even the prayers spoken on a whim. (Remember the picnic basket.)

3. See every answer to prayer as being a love sign directly from God to you. (Remember our precious baby.)
4. Take EVERYTHING to God in prayer.
5. Praise God for EVERYTHING.

———

I believe that God answers even my whimsical prayers because I spend a lot of time in prayer. I also spend a lot of time praising Him for everything I notice around me. God knows that His works will not be overlooked by me. I am as prone to wander into complacency as anyone else, so on that particular Thanksgiving Day in 2006, I prayed one extra-special prayer. I prayed that nothing God does in my life will be overlooked, but that He will continually receive my attention through the gift of praise.

Hebrews 13:15, *"By him therefore let us offer the sacrifice of praise to God continually, that is, the fruit of our lips giving thanks to his name."*

Hearing God's Voice

*T*HOUGH I HAD WRITTEN many articles for *Christian Womanhood* (a monthly magazine for Christian ladies) on looking for and seeing God, I had never written any articles on hearing God. In June of 2006, I decided to do so. The truth is, not only do I ask God to show Himself to me each day, but I also ask Him to speak to me each day. Allow me to share with you where this thought began.

As a teenager, I went through a stage where I was too analytical. Though I was blessed with a happy life, I fought a melancholy nature and could be extremely self-critical.

One Sunday night as a high school junior or senior, I was driving to church alone. I was disappointed in myself, and I began to plead for God to show me that He loved me. The following words "just happened to be" the choir special in that evening service:

"*I* stand amazed in the presence of Jesus the Nazarene
And wonder how He could love me, a sinner, condemned, unclean.
How marvelous! How wonderful! And my song shall ever be
How marvelous! How wonderful! Is my Saviour's love for me."

I'm sure this is a song I had heard many times before, but this time the words sounded different. For the first time that I can remember, I knew God was speaking directly to me, and I knew He loved me enough to orchestrate a love song for a specific need in my individual life. Since then, God and I have been enjoying a lifelong conversation.

Sometimes our conversation is more on the practical side. It seems that as soon as I say to God, "Now just where did I put my glasses?" He suggests one more place where I might look, and there they are! (We seem to be having more of these types of conversations since I hit 40!)

Sometimes our conversations are more physical. I hear God's voice in the chatter of our grandchildren, the singing of the birds, the tender words of a daughter when she says, "Mom, could we pray for that person's needs together now?"

I nearly always keep my office door open at the Christian Womanhood office, and I recognize the voice of each staff member. I hear God's voice in their kind, respectful words toward each other. I must be honest and say that fussing is not something I hear in the Christian Womanhood offices. I hear God's voice in the Marlene Evans' type of laughter that erupts from our managing editor, Jane Grafton, and in her occasional favorite exclamation—WAAAHOOOO! Allow me to interpret. This means something very good has just happened at the Christian Womanhood office.

I hear God's voice in the appreciative letters I receive from church members and Christian Womanhood subscribers. So often their letters come at a time when I am tempted to revert back to my self-critical ways. They refresh my spirit and help me to believe in my worth to God again.

I hear God's voice in my husband's exaggerated and oft-repeated comment, "You're the best!"

Sometimes God's voice brings a completely spiritual message. I hear Him as I hear my preacher preach. I feel loved, blessed, and convicted through almost every message, but I never wonder if my pastor husband is preaching to me. I hear God's voice clearly through messages, making it easy to accept rebuke from a pastor who is also my husband.

I hear God's voice through my daily Bible reading. Though I

use a manmade Bible reading plan, I find God must have whispered to its author what I would be needing on each day.

1. Ask God to speak to you and write down in a journal one thing He says to you each day. Each day I pray, "Jesus, please speak to me today and help me to hear You and to recognize You today."

2. Ask God to help you to hear Him, to listen to Him, and to obey Him. "…*To day if ye will hear his voice, harden not your hearts.*" (Hebrews 4:7) Many times I hear God saying things such as:

- "Cindy, tell your husband you are sorry."
- "Phone that hurting church member."
- "Put that in the offering plate."

I am not a very good Christian, but my heart is very tender toward God. My dad used to describe me as being tenderhearted. I never want to lose that quality. I know any time I disobey or ignore God's voice, I am hardening my heart toward Him. If you go on to read Hebrews 4, you will realize that listening to the voice of God is a prerequisite for rest or peace.

3. Use God's voice as a child-rearing tool. One of the most wonderful things about listening to God's voice is that when God speaks, miracles happen, and they are miracles that cannot be explained away. They are miracles that when shared can touch the heart of your children.

I have said that I do not know whether or not my children think I am a good mother. But I do believe they know that God is real in my life, and I do believe God is real to them.

4. Be aware of Who is speaking through you. I have heard some abrupt and difficult people proclaim, "That is just the way I am!" I so wish they would change—not for me, but for themselves. It is so wonderful to represent the voice of God through our conversations. If I could hear you talk among the people with whom you work, would I be able to hear God in your conversation anywhere?

When I speak or sing, I ask God to use every word in the heart of every person present in "great and mighty ways which I know not." That is a huge and impossible task for me, but not for Jesus. I believe He answers my prayer not because I am worthy, but because, for some strange reason, He loves to hear my voice as much as I love to hear His.

Singers or teachers, somewhere in your audience or classroom is a self-critical, melancholy teenager (or an adult) who wonders if God will put up with him. He needs someone to help him start a conversation with God. God could use your lesson, and God could use your song to speak to him. God is just waiting for you to ask Him to be involved.

5. Spend some time alone with God. I once heard it said that it is hard to hear a whisper if you are always in a room full of people talking. God's voice is often a whisper, but what He says is always worth hearing. God is longing for someone to listen to Him.

I am sure my husband has heard me cry out to God while I was sleeping or even awake around the house. I have seen my husband's mouth moving and have known he wasn't talking to me; he often talks to God in my presence. Are we crazy? No, we are living in reality. Our empty nest is not as empty as it may seem. There is a third Person involved in our conversations, and He is quite a talker!

If you are not on a conversational level with God, I pray that God will use this chapter to help you to hear His voice. I hope you can understand how dearly He loves you. He has so much He wants to tell you! Join me in my lifelong adventure of hearing the voice of God!

"...To day if ye will hear his voice, harden not your hearts." (Hebrews 4:7)

I Am God's Garden

"For we are labourers together with God: ye are God's husbandry, ye are God's building." (I Corinthians 3:9)

$\mathcal{M}$AY IS A MAGNIFICENT month to me because it is the month in which I plant a new garden. I have a landscaped area in the front of my house that is filled with perennials. Some time during the month of May, I also purchase several dozen annual flowers and plant them in baskets, flower pots, and flower boxes around my house.

If I get busy during the month of May and have to postpone my planting, I get a little edgy. When warm weather hits, I am a bit restless until my planting is complete. If I drive by Wal-Mart and see customers pushing shopping carts of flower flats to their cars, I become a little jealous and even more restless.

I go over in my mind what color scheme I will choose for my garden. Some years I decide to plant every color I can think of; that is my favorite color scheme. I count in my mind and sometimes walk around and measure to decide how much of what flower to put where.

Gardeners tell you to plant after ALL danger of frost is past. In Northwest Indiana, that is May 31. I can never wait; I plant my flowers when ALMOST ALL danger of frost is past. I plant them around Mother's Day each year, and so far I've been lucky. I count the days until I am available to plant.

During the summer months, I tend my flowers with care. I

water and fertilize them. I "dead head" them (remove their dead blooms), and I cut them back. Some I spray with bug killer. I hate to admit my vanity, but in the summer months I often drive very slowly past my house and stare at each flower from the road. I don't think my flowers or my garden would necessarily win a contest. But my garden is beautiful to me—because it is MY garden! I never tire of thinking of ways I could improve it for the next year.

I greet each blooming perennial as if it were an old friend I hadn't seen in a year—first the irises, then the lilacs, the potentilla and the roses, then the oriental lilies and the day lilies, then the black-eyed Susans and the hostas. Lastly, the fall mums are in bloom. I love to bend down and look very closely at each new bloom and praise my Creator for their beauty. What a variety He has created! I really, really love my garden. And then I was reading my Bible one day, and I came across I Corinthians 3:9.... I looked up the word *husbandry* and found it to mean "garden." I began to think, "I am God's garden!" I thought about how much I love my garden, simple though it might appear to others, and I understood anew how special I am to my God.

I also thought of how angry I feel when I see anything trying to destroy even one of my beautiful blooms. I hate Japanese beetles! Though normally I hate to watch anything die (I once hit a woodchuck with my car and cried all the way home), I am ruthless and heartless with a can of bug spray. I hate the fungus that sometimes shows up on the landscape bark in my garden! I immediately run for a shovel, scoop it out, and throw it away! I thought of how God must hate the sin that infests my life and begins to eat my soul. Though it may be a small sin, He knows the end result and wants to deal with it quickly. How God must long for me to hate the sin as much as He does!

I thought of how frustrated I became last summer with one rose bush that did not bear even one rose. I was so tempted to cut it down last year and put something more productive in its place.

I thought of how God must be frustrated with me when I don't bear fruit. Only He knows how much more beautiful I would be if I would replace that sin in my life with some fruit of souls won to Christ.

I thought of how much nurturing and care God bestows on me daily and how fragile I would be without His loving hand. I thought of the great opportunity I have to bring joy to God by yielding to His care, by shining forth with His beauty, and by turning my face to Him so He can see me for a while.

Most of all, I thought of how much God loves me—just because I am His! And He loves you too! Remember how special you are—you are God's garden!

That I May Appreciate Him

*P*HILIPPIANS 3:10 SAYS, "THAT I *may know him, and the power of his resurrection, and the fellowship of his sufferings, being made conformable unto his death.*" I used to wish that I could cry when I heard about the crucifixion of Christ. I have heard preachers, including my husband, describe Jesus' death in dramatic detail. I have listened to the cries around me in crowded auditoriums and been ashamed that I could not cry. I felt that I loved the Lord; I had a close walk with Him. Why could I not cry about such supreme sacrifice?

My first answer to my question came from Galatians 6:14: "*But God forbid that I should glory, save in the cross of our Lord Jesus Christ....*"

I resolved in my heart that it was okay for me to rejoice in what Jesus had done for me. I did not have to cry. I learned to rejoice in His sacrifice.

Then several years ago something happened that broke my heart for a while. I do not like to share my woes with others because God has provided me with such a wonderful life, but I do like to use my woes to help others with their heartbreaks. It seems that everyone has his heart broken at some time in his life.

At one point in my life, I felt rejected, betrayed, and misunderstood by some people—many of whom I still believe to be very

good people. Since then I can hardly ever sing about the crucifixion without tears coming to my eyes.

One day during my devotions, I was reading Philippians 3:10
in my John R. Rice Reference Bible. In the margin, I read that the
words "*that I may know him*" mean "that I may appreciate Him." It
is when we fellowship in the sufferings of Christ that we come, not
to just know what He did for us on the cross or to rejoice in what
He did for us, but we come to really appreciate what He did.

I am thankful for family, food, and freedom. I am thankful for
health and strength. I am thankful for hummingbirds, roses, and
yellow butterflies, but I am also thankful for suffering. I am not
particularly brave, and I don't wish to repeat any of the hurts that
I have known in the past, nor do I look forward to suffering in the
future. However, I do accept that suffering is a part of life, and I
am thankful for suffering because it causes me to appreciate what
Jesus did for me on the Cross.

I am thankful for sunshine, a lovely place to live, a wonderful
church, but I am also thankful for those people who have caused
me great pain in my life. Some are good people who at some point
in my life did what I'm afraid I may have also done to others. They
have brought tears to my eyes and caused me to feel the sting of
rejection, scorn, or misunderstanding. They have been tools in
the hand of the Lord to teach me not to take for granted the only
One Who really was unworthy of every bit of pain He bore. I am
thankful most of all for my Lord Jesus Christ. I am thankful:

- that He left His Father
- that He left His throne
- that He left Heaven
- that He was born on this earth
- that He lived in simplicity and poverty
- that He lived as a baby, a child, a teenager, a young adult
  and a middle-aged adult
- that He carried all of our griefs and sorrows

- that He knew what it was like to be rejected and left out
- that He suffered all of our temptations
- that He lived without sin
- that He gave us an example of how to live on this earth
- that He broke His heart for us
- that He broke His body for us
- that He shed his blood for us
- that He paid the price for our sins
- that He suffered our punishment
- that He rose again!!!!!!!!!!!!!!!!!!!
- that He protected me from many sins and addictions
- that He saved me from the many sins which I have committed.

As a child, I was blessed to come to know what He has done for me. As a teenager and a young adult, I learned to rejoice in what He has done for me. As a 47-year-old adult, I learned to appreciate what He has done for me.

My prayer is that we will not only know Who Jesus is, but that we will truly appreciate Him!

Step 2

Love With Christ's Love!

Rooted and Grounded in Love

*J*UNE 2004 WAS TRULY A special month for Brother Schaap and me as we celebrated our twenty-fifth wedding anniversary. We became husband and wife on June 1, 1979. What a wonderful choice I made on that day! I am very thankful for God's leading me to such a wonderful husband and to such a wonderful life! Ephesians 3:17-20 says, *"That Christ may dwell in your hearts by faith; that ye, being rooted and grounded in love, May be able to comprehend with all saints what is the breadth, and length, and depth, and height; And to know the love of Christ, which passeth knowledge, that ye might be filled with all the fulness of God. Now unto him that is able to do exceeding abundantly above all that we ask or think, according to the power that worketh in us."*

One day, while I was reading my Bible, those words in Ephesians 3 *"rooted and grounded in love"* jumped out at me. In Colossians 2:7, the Bible tells us that we are to be rooted and built up in God and in our walk with Him. *"Rooted and built up in him, and stablished in the faith, as ye have been taught, abounding therein with thanksgiving."* I wrote about this subject in my book *Living on the Bright Side.* I had read Ephesians 3:17 before but had never really thought about those words *"rooted and grounded in love."*

The words "rooted and grounded" cause me to think about the foundation upon which we stand. It also causes me to think about our innermost feelings about ourselves. I gleaned many truths from studying these four verses in Ephesians 3:17-20.

1. When we look into our hearts to establish our innermost opinion about ourselves, our self-identity if you please, that opinion should be based on love. It should not be based upon our talent, our intellect, or our physical appearance. It should not even be based on our good works. It should be based on how much we love others. For example:

- If asking, "What kind of a wife am I?" the answer should not be found in statements such as "I keep a clean house" or "I take good care of my appearance," but rather, "I really love my husband."
- If asking, "What kind of a mother am I?" the answer should not be found in statements such as, "I cook good meals," but rather, "I really love my children."
- If asking, "What kind of a Christian am I?" The answer should not be found in statements such as, "I have impeccable character," but rather, "I really love God and His people."

This is not my philosophy; it is the Bible's. The Word of God teaches that the platform we stand on in all of our relationships, in every aspect of our life, even in our relationship with our self, should be love.

2. It is not our own love which we should stand upon in our life and relationships; it is the love of God. The Bible says we are to "know the love of Christ." I would like my identity to be as someone who is "full of love." "She is full of love" is a compliment which I heard given to Joy Evans Ryder, the daughter of our Christian Womanhood founder, Marlene Evans. However, it is not Joy Ryder's love or Cindy Schaap's love that will be useful to or remembered by others. It is the love of Christ that must possess our hearts and our self-identity. I am confident that Joy Ryder is full of the love of Christ because it is only the love of Christ that can cause a woman made of flesh to be described as "full of love."

3. The only way one can be rooted and grounded in love is to know the love of Christ. We need to know how deep God's love is—deep enough to go down to the pit of Hell to redeem us. We need to know how broad God's love is—broad enough to reach all around the world. We need to know how high God's love is—high enough to reach to Heaven. And we need to know the length of God's love—it is eternal. Then we need to put that supernatural love deep in our hearts and let that be our platform upon which we stand. Let that type of love be the foundation of all of our relationships with others, and let that type of love be the foundation of our relationship with ourselves.

A couple of years ago, I began asking God to show His love to me each day. Each time I see Him, I say, "I see You, Jesus. I know You love me, and I love You, too!" I also have kept a journal, recording these events in which God showed His love for me. I also did a Bible study on love a few years ago. Since studying and looking for the love of God in my life, I do feel that I have come to love others more, even complete strangers.

4. When we are rooted in and know the love of Christ, God can do things in our lives that are "exceeding abundantly above all that we ask or think." The "power that worketh in us" to accomplish great things is the love of Christ.

God can use our marriage, our child rearing, our personal lives, and all of our relationships in ways that are far beyond what we ever imagined if we stand on the platform of God's love. If our hearts are full all the way from top to bottom with the love of Christ, God can use us in the lives of others in "great and mighty ways which we know not."

If you were to ask me, "Who are you, Mrs. Schaap? What is your identity that you lean upon for your self-worth? What makes you qualified for your position of service in God's work?" I would answer, "I am a person who walks with God." I may have little else to offer, but that is who I am.

If you were to ask me, "What do you want to be in the future, Mrs. Schaap?" I would have to answer, "I want to be a person who is full of the love of Christ." I am far from fitting that description, but that is my goal for the future.

It is the love of Christ in us that accomplishes things that are "exceeding abundantly above all that we ask or think." And it is God who gets the glory for all that we accomplish through His love. Ephesians 3:20, 21, *"Now unto him that is able to do exceeding abundantly above all that we ask or think, according to the power that worketh in us, Unto him be glory in the church by Christ Jesus throughout all ages, world without end. Amen."*

Loving Difficult People

I HAVE RECENTLY BEEN STUDYING the subject of love. I feel that this is the most needed attribute in my life. I have mentioned before that I do not regard the wife of a pastor as having a position with any kind of power, but rather a responsibility to love—all types of people.

Shortly after my husband became a pastor, I felt I could put most of our church members and our friends around the country into three categories:

1. There were those who I felt immediately embraced us as pastor and wife. These people took me in with open arms and gave me not only love, but also the admiration and respect that I did not deserve. It is, of course, easy to love this type of person, even when we know we did nothing to deserve their affection.

2. There were a few who rejected us. ALL of the members of First Baptist Church have been wonderful these past years. They have all displayed not only the greatness of our church people, but also the greatness of our miracle-working God. But our church is made of human beings, and human beings do not always accept change, especially when it revolves around the death of their pastor and the moving of their pastor's wife. I have been reminded in the past six years that I am a sensitive person, and yes, at times rejection hurt my spirit. I wish to share with you in this chapter how I handled it through the Lord's grace.

3. There were those who seemed reserved around us. They would never be unkind, but I felt they were letting us know they were skeptical about the heart of a younger pastor and wife. There was a part of my flesh that understood; I was also missing their pastor, who is my father, and their pastor's wife, who is my mother. Part of my flesh was hurt and even sometimes angry. Could they not understand that I was hurting too?

Then I remembered that God trusted my husband and me to love these people who were grieving the loss of my own father. I was to comfort them in my grief, AND I was to love them in my grief, even if I felt rejected in my grief; and (it gets harder) with a smile on my face!

I think my husband is better at this than I am. I am a very happy person, but I cannot hide my feelings easily. The asset is called transparency. The liability is called wearing your feelings on your sleeve. In this chapter, I would like to share with you how God helped me in spite of myself.

As a pastor's wife, I feel God wants me to love the rich and the poor, the comforting and the irritating, the builders and the competitors, and yes, even the sane and the not so sane. I also must love our educable slow member, Jack, even though he told me I look much fatter up close than I do far away! To be honest with you, over the last six years, I have felt full of love most of the time, so full of love that I want to hug all of our ladies and children in our church. (As a teenager, people who went around hugging people drove me crazy.) What has brought about this change in me?

Titus 3:1-6, *"Put them in mind to be subject to principalities and powers, to obey magistrates, to be ready to every good work."* (This verse reminds me that I am to be submissive, even to leaders who may reject me.)

"To speak evil of no man [even those who are downright mean], *to be no brawlers* [not a fighter], *but gentle, shewing all meekness unto all men."* (Even those who put me in my place?) When you think about it, God is asking an awful lot. Unless you leave out the "all men" part, which I have been very tempted to do. How in

the world can we keep this commandment to be submissive, gentle, and meek to all men?

Methods for Loving All Men

• Remember yourself at your most undeserving moment. Titus 3:3, *"For we ourselves also were sometimes foolish, disobedient, deceived, serving divers lusts and pleasures, living in malice and envy, hateful, and hating one another."* This verse describes me at my worst moment. When I act that way, I expect understanding and forgiveness from everybody, especially God. And the amazing thing is that I have received understanding and forgiveness from so many wonderful people, but especially from God. The completely self-sacrificial, perfect God of the universe gave me forgiveness and understanding at my worst and, yes, at my meanest moment. How can I do any less but give everyone I see His love and a big hug if it is appropriate?

• Bathe yourself in the love of God. Titus 3:4, *"But after that the kindness and love of God our Saviour toward man appeared."* I used to be a cool teenager who only liked those who fit perfectly into my cool zone. I used to make fun of weird people to get a laugh. People who were sappy and touchy used to drive me literally crazy. That was me at my worst. Allow to to rephrase Titus 3:4 for me personally. In other words, "…after that the kindness and love of God our Saviour toward ME appeared."

For the past two decades, I have been bathing myself in the love and forgiveness of God for me. I study His love, I look for His love, and I think about His love. I prayed for years for God to make me a more loving person; it did no good. I began to immerse myself in the love and forgiveness God had for me, and His love began to flow through me.

When I use perfume, I do not spray a dab on my wrists and neck. I spray it on my neck, on my wrists, my arms, my legs, and my clothes. I continue to spray it all day long. You may say that is wasteful, but at least I don't stink.

I love the new bath and body sets! I immerse myself in my new jacuzzi tub, add a little shower gel, and I am covered in a good scent. When I get out of the tub, I spray myself with the same scent, and my husband would tell you that I sometimes overdo it!

Some of you regard the love of God like an expensive perfume. You occasionally spray a dab of His love on you as you run out the door. All day long you try to function on a dab of love, and you stink in your relationships.

I am learning to immerse myself in the love of God. It is a precious ointment, too precious to waste, but it never runs out! My flesh still gets in the way sometimes, and I have a lot more to learn, but I am learning to love others. I exhort you, reader, to do the same. And may I also tell you that I love YOU! I may have never met you, but I do love you. Why? Because Jesus first loved me. *"We love him, because he first loved us."* (I John 4:19)

"Not by works of righteousness which we have done, but according to his mercy he saved us, by the washing [sounds like a good jacuzzi bath] *of regeneration, and renewing of the Holy Ghost. Which he shed on us **abundantly** through Jesus Christ our Saviour."* (Titus 3:5, 6)

Jesus is lavish in His giving of love, forgiveness, and mercy. I want to be the same! I never want to get over the exuberant joy of the love of God for that is the secret to my loving my husband, my family, all men, and YOU!

Step **3**

Know Your Enemy.

70 x 7

ONE OF THE MOST helpful lessons I ever learned, I learned through a sermon by my husband. It was a sermon on the three enemies of the Christian. In that sermon, he gave three enemies, their descriptions, and the weapons the Bible teaches we should use against them. In the next three chapters, I would like to elaborate on the following chart.

Enemy	Description	Weapon
Devil	The enemy who causes strife among the brethen; he accuses	The word of our testimony; resist the Devil
Flesh	The enemy who tries to get us to impress others	The Holy Spirit
World	The enemy that keeps us from doing God's will; materialism	Faith

The first enemy we fight is the Devil. God and the Devil are in a battle for every Christian's life. The Devil cannot have the eternal life of the Christian. My eternal life has been purchased by Jesus Christ on the cross, and I have accepted this gift that He purchased for me. Therefore, my eternal life is sealed up in God's storehouse.

But God and the Devil still battle for my earthly life. God wants me to live this life for Him so that I might earn rewards and influence others for His kingdom. The Devil wants to render my earthly life fruitless and ineffective. The battlefield where the Devil and God fight for my life is my mind.

Some days the oppression may be greater than others, but daily the Devil tries to put thoughts of strife in the Christian lady's mind. He accuses her husband by putting thoughts in her mind such as:

- "My husband is not as spiritual as I am."
- "My husband doesn't love me as much as he used to."
- "My husband doesn't treat me right."
- "My husband is not as great a man as the pastor."

What is the proper response to such critical thoughts about one's husband? "Jesus, I do not believe what the Devil is telling me. I will honor and respect my husband as the greatest man in the world."

Someone might ask, "But Mrs. Schaap, what if...?" Numerous statements could be used to fill in the blank, but I have studied the Bible, and I find only one clear-cut answer that is to be given to the critical thoughts the Devil places in a wife's mind toward her husband (and that's where they all come from.)

The proper response is to respect and honor her husband. A peaceful marriage is one where there is a wife who will not even get started with the Devil. She doesn't take even a moment to analyze the Devil's lies. She simply resists them by ignoring them.

James 4:7, *"Submit yourselves therefore to God. Resist the devil, and he will flee from you."* If we resist the Devil, he will leave us alone; but first we must submit ourselves to God. We submit ourselves to God by honoring and respecting our husband.

A woman who dishonors or disrespects her husband will have the Devil on her back constantly; he won't leave her alone. She will not understand that it is the Devil and why she can't get victory in her life. After all, she is more spiritual than her husband. (Says who?)

I have had countless women come to my office and tell me

what heathens their husbands are. I have seen those same wives begin to honor and respect their husband and then tell me how wonderful their husband is. The Devil caused them to be very convinced of a lie that brought them misery. Honoring and respecting their husbands caused them to find freedom and victory over that lie. They began to see their husbands through the light of truth—human and imperfect as all humans are, yet full of potential that can be brought to life through the wife's obedience to God in honoring and respecting her husband.

Revelation 12:11a, "*And they overcame him by the blood of the Lamb, and by the word of their testimony....*" It is the word of our testimony or our praise to God that overcomes the Devil. A wife's praise for her husband overcomes the Devil in her marriage.

- "I am so thankful that I am not divorced."
- "I am so thankful that I have a provider."
- "I am so thankful to God that my husband is in his prime and God is using him."
- "I am committed to God's truth for my life that my husband is the best man in the world for me."
- "Praise the Lord for a husband who loves me."

The Devil also tries to fight us by putting critical thoughts in our minds about our brothers and sisters in Christ.

- "Susie is backslidden."
- "Mary's daughter should not be at a state university."
- "Lori spends too much money."

Even if such thoughts are true, the proper response is: "Jesus, I know that You don't want critical [devilish] thoughts to fill my mind today. I will ignore what the Devil is saying to me."

What about thoughts of past hurts, especially the deeply wounding ones? I believe that is why the Bible commands us to forgive our neighbor 70 x 7 times. That is enough forgiveness for every day of the year and more.

When I am alone and the Devil tries to put thoughts in my

mind such as "Don't forget how hurtful and cruel that person was to you," I respond by saying: "Jesus, I forgive that person again today."

I resist the Devil and fill my thoughts with things for which I have to be thankful. Sometimes I even take a few moments to reflect on the positive qualities of the person who hurt me.

We don't have victory in our lives because we don't even recognize our enemy. Perhaps we think our enemy is our husband's weaknesses or the marriage contract in which we are stuck. The real enemy is the Devil. He is the one who accuses and sows strife. By resisting him with the word of our testimony, we can have both a peaceful marriage and a peaceful life.

My Enemy—Myself

ONE OF THE THREE enemies of the Christian lady is her flesh. This is the enemy that causes her to want to be selfish and to impress others. Since every lady is made of flesh, every woman has this enemy.

I am made of flesh, and the flesh nature is sinful. Because it is sinful, my flesh nature is not growing more spiritual. Flesh cannot be spiritual. My flesh is growing weaker every day. I have in me (as do you, I might add) a desire to be selfish, to get my own way, and to impress others. My flesh wants to be better than you—have the nicest dress, the prettiest face, the best house, and so forth. My flesh left to itself will end up alone—a miserable old lady who has no love or influence on anyone.

However, when Jesus ascended into Heaven, He knew I would need someone to help me gain the victory—over me. So He left me a dear, precious Friend—the Holy Spirit.

The Holy Spirit can do amazing things through me. He can put down my flesh and cause me to be spiritual. With the Holy Spirit's help, my spirit can actually be growing stronger and sweeter every day. The Holy Spirit alone is the One Who can cause me to be unselfish, to want another's way, and to love and bless others. The Holy Spirit through me wants others to have a nice dress, a pretty face, and a beautiful house. The Holy Spirit does not seek the best for self. He seeks the best for others.

A fleshly wife will not wait on her husband; she finds it humiliating and tiring.
A Spirit-filled wife will find great freedom, victory, and joy in waiting on her husband.

A fleshly wife will only follow her husband if he agrees with her, and they will rarely agree.
A Spirit-filled wife will submit to her husband's wishes when she doesn't feel agreement.

A fleshly mother will leave her children or ignore them because they are an inconvenience.
A Spirit-filled mother will stay committed to the cause of training her children for the sake of her children.

A fleshly mother will become angry when her adult children leave her out of something she wanted to be a part of.
A Spirit-filled mother will be glad that her adult children are happy and will not make herself the issue.

A fleshly church member will go to church to show off a new outfit and will get angry if she is overlooked for a position.
A Spirit-filled church member will go to church to serve and to encourage others.

I could go on, but I think you get my point. Let me add that I have lived my life in both the flesh and the Spirit. I have lived in all of the above-mentioned mind sets, and I find that true victory and joy come to the Spirit-filled Christian lady.

Ephesians chapters 5 and 6 teach us mainly two things: how to be Spirit-filled and how to get along with others. If you are not Spirit-filled, you will not be able to get along with others. Your

flesh will prohibit that! How then can we be filled with the Spirit?
1. Read the Bible and pray daily.
2. Ask for forgiveness of sins and for the Holy Spirit to fill you several times a day.
3. Listen to sermon tapes.
4. Listen to praise music.
5. Read and sing hymns and spiritual songs.
6. Underline verses in your daily Bible reading and read them again through the day.
7. Do things for others.
8. Go soul winning.
9. Stay away from things that include the sins listed in Ephesians 4:25-31.

I have nothing to offer the people with whom I work except sinful flesh. But I have a dear gift from God—His Holy Spirit. When He fills me, wonderful things happen. Extraordinary things take place like the building of a happy marriage, the rearing of good children, the strengthening of family relationships, and the blessing of my fellow church members.

Don't forget to get the victory over your own worst enemy—you. Don't forget to use your greatest weapon—the precious Holy Spirit of Jesus Christ!

Seek Ye First

*W*HEN MY HUSBAND AND I had been married a couple of years, I went to him and asked him if we could look for a new house. Several of our peers were upscaling, and I was getting the "bug" to do the same. I was ignorant of the fact that I was doing battle with one of the three enemies of the Christian—the world.

I remember my husband's response clearly. "Cindy, we will never seek material things in our lives. This is a nice house, and we will stay in it until God kicks us out."

I went back to my ironing that I had been doing previously and told the Lord that I knew my husband was right and that I would follow him. I'm sure I felt disappointed, but mainly I recall feeling very secure.

Several months later, though I had never spoken my request to anyone else, God clearly "kicked us out and into" another house. Some church members, because of a financial need, wanted to sell their house. My dad, who was our pastor, told us that he did not think we would want to stay indefinitely in the house where we were living. He told us he thought it was time that we find something permanent. He recommended the house for sale by our church member. I remember driving in the driveway, seeing my dream house, and marveling at the fact that God knew my taste even better than I did.

Not long after moving into our house, I was given a plaque with the verse Matthew 6:33, "*But seek ye first the kingdom of God, and his righteousness; and all these things shall be added unto you.*" I placed the plaque on the fireplace mantel of our new home along with a family picture. Many nights I turned off the lights in the living room and paused to look at that verse and the picture of our family. I thanked God that when we did seek Him first, more than we could have expected was added to us.

A very lovely Christian lady tried to get me to go into a secular business. Truthfully, I was very tempted. As a young married lady, there were so many things I couldn't afford after the groceries were bought. I could rise up the ladder in business and have many nice, impressive things. I did not know it then, but my enemy, the world, was working on me. After some thought, I decided that I should use any extra time in a way that would draw me closer to my husband. The next year I began teaching very part-time at Hyles-Anderson College instead.

As I look back over the decisions my husband and I have made in our marriage, I do not see his decision to candidate for the pastorate as one of the most important. I don't think either one of us felt there was a decision to be made at that time. We felt the Lord had opened a door, and we had to walk through it. I believe the two decisions I have already shared in this article were two of the most important. Why?

1. Because they were made at the beginning of our marriage, and the foundation of a marriage establishes what the rest of the marriage will be.
2. Because if we had not made the right decision regarding the world at these two times, I do not think my husband would have been in the place he needed to be to accept the pastorate of First Baptist of Hammond.

What is the world? The world is materialism and the things that would stop us from doing God's will. How do we fight the world? We fight it through faith. I John 5:4 says, *"For whatsoever is born of God overcometh the world: and this is the victory that overcometh the world, even our faith."* Faith that believes in Matthew 6:33 will prevent us from succumbing to materialism. We don't have to believe that God will give us our dream house. He may not choose to do that. We just need to believe that God has an "all-these-things" plan for our life and that it is God's will—not the world—that will make us happy.

God commands us not to love the world, neither the things that are in the world. I still fight my old enemy, the world. Nicer things and more money still like to call my name. When they call my name, I like to quote a verse that is really easy to memorize: Luke 17:32, "Remember Lot's wife."

I'm sure I am more materially spoiled than I realize. But I do not believe that my husband has had to sacrifice any of God's will in order to provide for me. I have not had to manipulate or connive to get the nice things that God has provided.

At this writing more than 20 years later, we still live in that little dream house. God just never kicked us out. Has my dream house made me happy? Not really. Though I love my home, I have had days where I felt it was not good enough and that I would sell it to the lowest bidder. Then I got my attitude right and became thankful for my house again. What has made me happy are the ways God has used my husband and me.

Not long ago our church family moved into one of the most beautiful auditoriums I have ever seen. That made me happy. Just a few minutes ago our subscription manager, Janice Wolfe, poked her head in my office door and told me that my husband had been responsible for the salvation of two souls today. That made me happy!

When I was a young girl, I thought the "all these things" was my dream house, a nice wardrobe, a car, and so forth. At 47, I realize that the "all these things" are much more than that. They are the souls we have won and the way God has used us. God's will is what has made us happy.

Disclaimer: I am not saying that one should never buy a bigger house, nor am I saying a full-time Christian worker's wife should never work a secular job. I am also not saying that I am the judge of when such decisions should be made. I believe it is the how and the why of such decisions that are important. And as my dad often reminded me, "Never make a decision based on money alone." Some other good should come as a result of the decision. I deem it important to share these thoughts because I have seen many a man leave a ministry shortly after his wife became successful in a secular career. I have also seen the opposite. The decision is between you, your husband, and God and should be based on God's will.

May God give you the victory over the world, the flesh, and the Devil through faith, the Holy Spirit, and the word of your testimony!

Step 4

Be Discreet!

How to Be Discreet

I USE TITUS 2:4 AND 5 FOR all of my marriage curriculum in the "Christian Womanhood" class I teach at Hyles-Anderson College. *"That they may teach the young women to be sober, to love their husbands, to love their children, To be discreet, chaste, keepers at home, good, obedient to their own husbands, that the word of God be not blasphemed."*

Week one I teach the girls how to be sober, week two I teach the girls how to love their husbands, and so forth. Some time around the fourth week of the class, I teach the girls what I have learned about how to be discreet. I bring into class a large picture of a pig that has just finished rolling in the mud. I take off one of my earrings and clip it to the pig's ear on the picture. I sarcastically ask the girls to notice how much more attractive the pig is with the earring on its ear.

Then I remind them of Proverbs 11:22 which says, *"As a jewel of gold in a swine's snout, so is a fair woman which is without discretion."* I remind the girls that the most beautiful of women is really not attractive at all once you get to know her, if she does not possess discretion.

I would like to introduce this chapter by defining the word *discretion.* I used to think that *discretion* was a word that alluded to purity. This is partly true, but the word *discreet* means much more than that. The Bible word *discreet* is sometimes interpreted to mean "having common sense." Another good Bible interpretation is "minding your own business." In other words, the woman who has learned the discipline of discretion has learned the discipline of boundaries. She knows how to stay within her own boundaries.

My mother has been a wonderful example of Bible discretion all of her years as a pastor's wife. She and my dad, as well as my husband, have answered many questions for me through the years which have helped me learn to grow in the Bible discipline of discretion.

In my study of discretion, I have learned several practical things that have been a help and of which I have found myself needing to be reminded every time my husband has had a change in his ministry.

1. Do not give your advice to your husband unless you are asked. My husband often asks for my advice, and I often give it. But I have trained myself not to give opinions where I might have a tendency to interfere.

For example, I rarely give advice to my husband about his sermons. When he was a young man, he sometimes would ask my advice about which of two sermons he should preach. I usually said, "Either one would be fine; I'm sure you'll make the best choice." I have always tried to avoid giving advice about my husband's sermons because I know this is an area where I might have a tendency to interfere. The Holy Spirit should show a man what to preach. I don't believe that the Holy Spirit uses the wife to show her husband what or even how to preach.

No one feels more vulnerable about her husband's preaching than the wife. Why? Because a wife and her family are very exposed when their own flesh and blood is speaking before a congregation. Because of this, a wife would be more prone to find something that she wishes her husband had not said. A statement taken in stride by the audience might be taken more sensitively by the pastor's wife. If a wife is not careful, she will frequently criticize her husband's preaching. I **hate** this statement: "My wife is my best critic." Where is that philosophy taught in the Bible?

If my husband asks my advice about a situation in the church, I might give my advice. But I keep a predetermined attitude that I will not become strong-willed about my advice to my husband. And I frequently remind him that I am only giving my opinion and have no desire to take part in making the decision.

2. Do not give unnecessary advice to teenage and adult children. This was also hard for me to learn. I love to philosophize, and I am a teacher. Because of this, I enjoyed teaching my small children. It was a startling thing the first time that I learned that my sweet teenage daughter did not want a lecture about every subject she began. Surely she was in a stage of rebellion...or was she?

I learned that my teenage daughter did not need me to be constantly advising her about every little dating experience and so forth. Every fun time didn't need to turn into another training session from Mom. Instead, I needed to learn to listen and to wait until the timing was right for philosophizing. I also needed to keep building a fun and loving relationship so that my daughter would ask me questions when she needed help.

3. Don't give advice to friends and other individuals unless you are asked. I once had a friend who made a decision that was dead wrong, not sinful, but unwise. Because this friend had read my books, I believe she knew I thought she was wrong. She tried to justify her action to me. I did not argue with her. I merely listened. Why? Because I have learned, sometimes the hard way, that people seldom heed unsought advice. It usually does more harm than good.

Also, I have learned that it is not right or discreet to give unsought advice. So I strive to mind my own business. I do give advice to a general audience when I speak or write; that is an advantage that a writer or speaker has. But I do not write books or give speeches with one person in mind. I will not give unsought advice in this way because I do not know the whole story of those to whom I write. Therefore, I do not know what is best. I write to correct negative trends that I have noticed among many people. Most of all, I write to correct myself.

Through the years, I have had some people call and ask me to fly to other states to try to talk a wife into going back to her husband. I have always refused. Why? Because this wife was not asking for my advice; her friend was.

This principle may seem almost cold and heartless, but I have been in the ministry long enough to see the Devil wreak havoc through women who do not know how to remain quiet when their advice is not being sought. How in the world does a woman keep her mouth shut when she knows someone is making a big mistake?

- How about trying prayer?
- How about trying lots of fervent intercessory prayer and maybe even fasting?
- How about believing in the power of God being greater than your own?

I guarantee you that praying women are discreet women.

Do you remember the jewel of gold in a swine's snout? Let's not just work on our appearance daily; let's work on not giving our advice or opinion when it is unsought. It will be hard, but I imagine with a lot of practice, you and I could become really good at it.

4. Don't give advice if you don't know the answer. As a counselor, don't be afraid to use the words "I don't know" when necessary.

5. Don't correct problems without seeking your husband's permission. If I have a "bone to pick" or a problem to correct with another person, I ask my husband whether I should deal with it or leave it alone.

Sometimes my husband advises me to go to the appropriate person and to discuss the subject with her. As my authority and as a person standing at a different angle from the problem, my husband has wisdom that I don't. If his wisdom tells him that it would be appropriate and helpful for me to confront an issue, then I do so.

Several times in my life, however, my husband has told me to "leave it alone." Again, as my authority and as a person looking from the outside into my life, he sees things I do not see. He may see that I am just having a bad day. He may see that I am crossing a boundary line and entering into a zone where I do not belong. He may see that the person with whom I am dealing is unreasonable, and the situation cannot be corrected without hurt to one or both parties. Many times my husband will care for the problem himself by taking it to the appropriate authority in an effort to protect my spirit from being involved in a "mess."

Remember, when we as wives become involved in problems that hurt us, it is usually our husband who has to catch our tears. He sometimes has to clean up the human relationship messes which we create. I do not mind asking my husband to help in an area where he has advised me to become involved. However, it is not fair for him to have to fix problems that he would have wanted me to avoid in the first place.

Consider Proverbs 27:15, 16, which says, *"A continual dropping in a very rainy day and a contentious woman are alike. Whosoever hideth her hideth the wind, and the ointment of his right hand, which bewrayeth itself."*

In my John R. Rice Reference Bible, the word *hideth* in verse 15 is interpreted "keeps her out of things." It is a good idea to keep a woman out of things which are not her business. Much of our feelings of anger and contention are unnecessary. They come from getting involved in things which are none of our business. How do we keep from becoming involved in things which are none of our business? We learn to be discreet.

6. Do not correct where you do not have authority. For

example, I had authority over my own two children. Therefore, I corrected them if they needed to be corrected. But I rarely correct others' children. I do not watch in the services or in the hallways of church to see whose children I can correct. If I see blatant misbehavior and there is no one else around to correct it, I would handle it myself. If there is a man around (such as an usher in the church) when I see misbehavior, I will most likely ask him to care for the situation.

I do not look for people to correct. I do not relish in informing people about their children's misbehavior. I would not call parents about their child's misbehavior without asking my husband's advice. I would only call if he advised me to do so.

This is especially good advice for a pastor's wife. Following this advice can keep the pastor's wife from becoming the "dragon lady" or the "enforcer" of the church. It can prevent people problems which can put stress upon the wife and, therefore, add stress to her marriage. If you are a person who likes to correct problems, this principle is especially good to follow.

Several years ago, I received a note from about five rows behind me in our church auditorium. It was from a lady telling me that there was a piece of lint on my husband's jacket. I checked it out and found a very minuscule piece of lint. I chose not to correct it. Why? Because I do not correct someone unless the embarrassment of the mistake is greater than the embarrassment of the correction. My goal is to show my respect to my husband, not to be sure that he and I are perceived as faultless. A person who is more concerned about respecting others than she is about showing her authority will not correct unless the correction is necessary.

As a teacher at Hyles-Anderson College, I have authority in my classroom. I have confidence in that authority and do not hesitate to keep classroom control. However, because I have confidence in my authority, I do not need to "push my weight around" in the classroom. Because of this, if there is a conflict in the classroom, I usually refer to the rule book or to the English faculty (when I am teaching English) to enforce the rules. I do not make statements like, "I'll have you know that I am in charge here, and this is the way I want things done."

Instead I say things like, "The English faculty has decided that we must do it this way," or "The rule book says that we must do it this way." Making these kinds of statements keeps me from being bossy toward the young men, and it helps me to set a good example for the young ladies. I want my students to learn that a lady can do a job well without sacrificing femininity or leaving her proper role.

If I see a person breaking a rule outside of my classroom, I handle things differently. I am now outside of my classroom, and I am outside of my own personal realm of authority. Therefore, I take rule infractions to the proper authority, and I let them handle them. If I have a question about an infraction, I ask my husband's advice first. Getting his perspective prevents me from being the pastor's wife enforcer of Hyles-Anderson College. It also prevents me from being disrespectful toward a young man at the college. I do not think that a lady should ever be bossy or disrespectful toward a young man.

I do, however, believe that the rules of a college or a school should be upheld. A rule is not really a rule unless it is enforced. There is a proper and an improper way for a lady to enforce rules. All authority should remember that a rule should be enforced with respect and remember that according to Acts 10:34, "...*God is no respecter of persons.*" The same respect should be shown to each person who breaks each rule.

I am in no way trying to set myself up as the perfect example. Some of these things I have learned the hard way. Everyone profits when respect and discretion are a part of our daily lives. The one who profits the most is the person who shows the discretion.

That person will be able to live in harmony with others and will prevent stress in his or her own life.

It is a good feeling to know that we are handling the people problems in our lives in a way that pleases the Lord and in a way that keeps us within the boundaries that God has set for us. Remember, boundaries are for our own protection. Let's live within the boundaries that God has set for us. Life within those boundaries can be very easily lived!

7. **Ignore evil forebodings.** I have a pretty strong intuition about some things. I once visited a church where my husband was preaching. A visiting preacher came to the front and shook my hand. When he did, I looked in his eyes, and my intuition told me that man was struggling morally. Shortly thereafter, that man had to leave his church because of moral problems. I suppose most of us have some similar story we could tell.

Does this experience cause me to act upon my intuition? No! An intuition can be correct, but an intuition can also be a very deceitful tool which is used of the Devil. I may have an evil foreboding because I actually see evil. Or I may have an evil foreboding because I am overly tired or had too much pepperoni pizza before I went to sleep. A discreet woman will ignore her intuition most of the time and will base her decisions upon the truth of God's Word.

8. **Don't investigate your suspicions.** When I thought I saw a morally troubled man, did I tell my husband? No! I did not tell my husband because I had no facts to back up my intuition. I also did not tell my husband because it would not affect us, and therefore, it was none of my business.

I believe the Devil often uses an indiscreet woman in the church to stir up trouble. How does he do this? He gets her to believe in something evil. It may be the truth, or it could just as well be a lie, because the Devil is the father of lies.

Often sincere women get caught up in investigating and trying to prove evil exists. Many times these women really believe there is a sin that genuinely needs to be fixed. The problem lies in the fact that the investigation is none of the woman's business. It is probably a tool of the Devil to distract her from her own Christian growth, her own husband, and her own children. The Devil also uses this as a tool to wreak havoc in many churches. No wonder the book of Proverbs warns us of indiscreet women!

I have heard of people setting up traps so they can catch someone in his wrongdoing. This is a great idea if you are a private detective. But if you are a wife and/or a mother, it is a foolish waste of time you could be using to care for your family or pray for your church.

9. Practice mind control. The key to ignoring evil forebodings and not investigating suspicions is practicing mind control. This is a concept that was taught repeatedly by Mrs. Marlene Evans. I am forever grateful to her for that. Mind control takes place when we take everything to the Lord. We can tell Him our intuitions, our forebodings, as well as the facts; then we can ask Him to care for them. God's power is great enough to solve any church problem—even those which are beyond our control and none of our business.

After we pray, we can train our mind to practice Philippians 4:8 thinking. *"Finally, brethren, whatsoever things are true, whatsoever things are honest, whatsoever things are just, whatsoever things are pure, whatsoever things are lovely, whatsoever things are of good report; if there be any virtue, and if there be any praise, think on these things. Those things, which ye have both learned, and received, and heard, and seen in me, do: and the God of peace shall be with you."* We can keep our minds busy thinking of only spiritual and positive things, perhaps through the use of sermon CDs, praise music, and so forth.

10. Pray about any matter that irritates you. It is especially easy for a person who is inexperienced at counseling to feel intimidated when he or she doesn't know the answer. A discreet woman will realize how important it is **not** to give wrong advice. Though I have been doing some counseling for many years now, I do not look for people to counsel. Telling people what to do is not something I relish. When I am counseling, I do not hesitate to say if I do not know the answer. There are certain situations in counseling with which I have had little experience. If such a situation arises, I do not hesitate to refer the counselee to another counselor. A pastor's wife can save her husband much heartache by not giving advice if she does not know the answer.

Also, when I am counseling, I make sure I understand the question which is being asked. I may listen to the counselee and hear things which cause me to be tempted to give unsought advice. Because of this, I allow those with whom I counsel to talk for several minutes. Next I ask them to phrase to me their specific question. Then I proceed to answer only the question given.

Another good point of discretion is not to answer unnecessary questions. In my travels, I have heard of groups of ladies in churches arguing over issues which should not even be discussed.

For example, controversies regarding the physical relationship in marriage should not be discussed among women. More than once, someone has tried to get my advice about such controversies. I try to respond politely, but I always respond in a manner similar to this: "That is a matter which should only be discussed between a husband and wife. Therefore, you and I have no obligation to answer such questions to anyone else." To think of a group of women arguing on such a matter causes me to picture a bunch of pigs squirming and squealing in the mud.

The answer to all indiscretion is to pray about everything that irritates you. I guarantee you that a woman who is often indiscreet is not a praying woman. Though I have many weaknesses, I believe that one of my strengths is my ability to be honest with God. If someone hurts me, I tell the Lord. If something makes me angry, I tell the Lord. Then I ask the Lord to help my attitude about the problem and to fix the problem as is His will.

I also try to wait 24 hours before taking a problem to my husband. A loving husband will sometimes become angry when his wife is mistreated. I could abuse my position as a pastor's wife by recklessly taking people problems in the church to my husband. I try to avoid being a hindrance in this way by keeping my prayer life strong and consistent. I ask the Lord what He would have me to take to my husband.

I practiced this same principle when I was the pastor's daughter. I did not take my problems with other church members to my dad. I did not want to use my position as the pastor's daughter to abuse other church members' relationships with their pastor. I fear God too much to treat God's people in such an unkind manner.

Of course, I have not been perfect in any of these areas, and I have learned many things about discretion the hard way. But it seems that as my discretion has grown, so has my peace of mind. It is my desire to see that same peace of mind to spread through all of the fundamental homes and churches in our nation. Let's remember to mind our own business and to leave it at that!

The result of living the life of a discreet woman is found in Philippians 4:7, *"And the peace of God, which passeth all understanding, shall keep your hearts and minds through Christ Jesus."* Discreet living is happy living. May yours be the happiest!

Being a "Gracious Woman Who Retaineth Honor"

*F*OR YEARS I HAVE watched my mother, Mrs. Jack Hyles, maintain what I call a "gracious reserve" between herself and members of the opposite sex. Her ability to be gracious and friendly and yet never in any way to be indiscreet has often amazed me, especially because she has always been so beautiful. (It was not unusual for my mother to receive some compliment from a strange man as we were shopping together, etc. At times, this was quite an ego-buster for my sisters and me.)

I have tried to put down in writing just what it means to have a "gracious reserve." Please allow me to share some of these ideas with you.

1. **Look a man in the eyes only.** Not only should you look a man in the eyes, but you should keep a discreet look in your eye. I still cannot exactly describe what a look of discretion is, but I have seen what it is not. Maybe just being aware of how we are coming across will help a girl to look at a man in the proper way.

2. **Maintain a safe distance between yourself and a man when you are talking with him.** A safe distance will keep a short girl from looking up at a taller man as if she has just been struck by lightning.

3. **Talk to a man in a courteous, but formal tone of voice.** There should be a definite difference in the tone of voice a wife

uses with her husband and the one she uses with other men.

4. **Maintain good posture when talking with other men.** I may stand slouchy and "cute" when I am talking to my husband, but I would not want to do that with someone else's husband lest I give a wrong impression.

5. **When greeting a married couple, always acknowledge the wife first.** Also, when you are conversing with a couple, include the wife in the conversation as much as possible.

6. **Never follow a man with your eyes after he has passed you.** I have seen some young girls get so excited about passing a married man whom they admired that they practically fell apart emotionally. Surely a lady can learn to make a man feel welcome and respected without causing him (or his wife) to have a cardiac arrest.

7. **Never ride alone in a car with a man.** I take it a step further and never allow myself to be the only lady in a car full of males, unless my husband is one of them.

8. **Never compliment a man about his appearance.** One may tell a good male friend in the presence of his wife that she likes his tie. That would be very different from saying, "Wow! You sure look nice today."

9. **Other than a handshake, I believe touching members of the opposite sex is unnecessary.** (This does not include members of the immediate family.)

10. **Of course, suggestive conversation is always inappropriate—even in jest.**

11. **Shower your preacher with lots of gifts and notes of praise, but include his wife in all your thoughtful deeds.** As soon as my husband and I became engaged, I made it a practice never to write a man telling him how much I enjoyed his preaching without also including my fiance's name on the note .

12. **Don't counsel with men about sexual problems.** Also be careful about counseling with any man on a regular basis, in a secluded area, or late at night.

13. It is my opinion that it is unwise for a woman to allow someone other than her husband to depend too heavily on her. For example, a secretary should not also be the baby sitter for her boss's children, errand runner for her boss's wife, etc. Tragedy often happens when a secretary becomes like "just another member of the family."

14. Last but not least, sow what you want to reap. Sometimes single girls may be too friendly with married men, thinking they have nothing to lose. However, if the Biblical law of sowing and reaping is accurate, then she has everything to lose. I tell my students at Hyles-Anderson College to "treat other women's husbands the way you want yours to be treated" because that is exactly what will happen.

Proverbs 22:3 says, "*A prudent man forseeth the evil, and hideth himself: but the simple pass on, and are punished.*" Let's take advance precautions to prevent disaster in the lives of ourselves, those about whom we care, and God's people.

One more thing—**thank you, Mom, for being a "*gracious woman who retaineth honor*"** and also for being graciously reserved. This has revealed to me that you truly are a beautiful lady.

Step 5

Overcome
Depression!

Posttrauma Depression

ELIJAH CALLED DOWN FIRE from Heaven. In I Kings 18 he fought and won a great spiritual battle. He put himself on the spot in front of King Ahab and many of the liberals of his day. He put God on the spot in front of the most wicked people alive, and God came through for Him in a big way. What a man, and what a victory! Yet in I Kings 19, we discover a different type of man. It is almost like watching Dr. Jekyll and Mr Hyde.

Elijah was threatened by Queen Jezebel. Although he was not threatened by King Ahab and the liberals in I Kings 18, he was threatened by one woman in I Kings 19. (Everyone knows that one angry woman can be very scary!) The Bible says that Elijah ran away, sat down under a tree, and told God he wanted to die. Every preacher's wife needs to know that one of the most vulnerable times of a Christian's life is right after a great spiritual battle.

First Baptist Church of Hammond went through a great battle in 1984 and again in 1989. I remained steady. Though victory came in our battles, I still found myself depressed a few years later. I had lost many friends during our battles. I sat down under my spiritual tree of depression and noticed that in the process of time, my trust had been severely damaged. God was with me as I experienced several months of a great spiritual valley, where Jesus taught me to trust again.

Allow me to share with you from Elijah's story some solutions to the problem of posttrauma depression.

1. **Rest is often the #1 need of the spiritually depressed.** A wise preacher's wife should guard her rest. Also recognize that after great spiritual battles, there is a need for extra rest. When you notice you are depressed, plan seasons of extra rest.

During the 2004 Youth Conference, over 1,000 young people surrendered to the mission field after one of my husband's sermons. I cannot tell you how weary my husband and I felt for weeks to come. I had done little else but carry my husband to the Lord in prayer and share his burden, yet I was exhausted, and he, of course, even more so. I struggled a little more than usual for a few weeks as I sought to balance my emotions with extra badly needed rest.

Rest is a key factor in balancing emotions. I usually take a 30-minute nap each afternoon so that I can be fresh during the evening hours when I get to spend most of my time with my husband. I Kings 19:5, *"And as he lay and slept under a juniper tree, behold, then an angel touched him, and said unto him, Arise and eat."*

2. **Proper nutrition is needed to fight depression.** The second thing Elijah did after he rested was to eat and drink. He did this in obedience to the command of an angel.

Many people handle their desire to lose weight and their problems using the feast-or-famine method. They eat nothing for much of the day until they are so starved that they are willing to eat anything. I have counseled many hyper, out-of-control women who, when I asked them, informed me that they had not had anything to eat for several hours. Many have not had a decent meal for days. A hungry stomach leaves us not only crabby, but also malnourished and agitated.

Unless I am fasting, I try to eat a small amount of protein every two hours, usually just enough to fit in the palm of my hand. I also count my intake of fruits and vegetables each day. I make sure I have my "five-to-thrive" servings of fruits and vegetables, but some doctors are now saying to eat nine or more servings each day. If you have not been eating fruits and vegetables daily, start with the "five-to-thrive" plan.

Because our food is not as rich in vitamins as it once was, I also believe in taking food supplements. Some supplements that I believe can help a woman's spirit are the following:

- Vitamin E (1,000 mg/day)
- Spirulina (a blue-green algae product filled with B vitamins)
- Multi-vitamin
- Vitamin B-6 (200 mg/day)
- Magnesium (400 mg/day)
- Calcium (1,000 mg/day)
- Evening Primrose Oil (1,000 mg/day)

Many other options are available, but the key is to study your own body and learn what you need to keep your spirit level. I consult with both the nutritionist at my local health food store and with a Christian nurse. Some herbs are billed as giving energy that can be harmful to the body, so it is always a good idea to study carefully and to get a second opinion about any unfamiliar supplements. Also, if you have a chronic illness, your doctor should be consulted first. Be slow to trust just one medical opinion, especially if it is a non-Christian opinion.

I strive to drink between 64 and 72 ounces of water daily. When I drink considerably less, I immediately notice a decline in both my physical and emotional well-being.

Moderation is a key in seeking to eat healthy. The Bible says we are to eat in faith the food that is set before us. We can't always control every bite that goes into ours and our children's mouths, nor should we try to control our husbands. Romans 14:23, *"And he that doubteth is damned if he eat, because he eateth not of faith: for whatsoever is not of faith is sin."* We cannot live our lives in fear of something that is less than organic entering our mouths. We also should be sensible and spiritual in our food choices. I do not believe God intended us to indulge ourselves in empty calories that contain more chemicals than they do real food. Moderation is a key word in proper nutrition. Philippians 4:5, *"Let your moderation be known unto all men. The Lord is at hand."*

I believe in trying rest, proper nutrition, and supplements first, as well as exercise. Try as many practical things as you can first. Then if the depression is still ongoing, a doctor should be seen and a sound medical check-up should take place, checking things like hormones, thyroid, and so forth.

I have found in my own life that problems are best corrected by seeking both spiritual solutions and practical solutions. If both types of solutions are not sought, the problem will probably go unsolved.

3. Walking with God is needed to fight depression. In I Kings 19:9-18, Elijah begins a dialogue with God. Notice that God did not first handle Elijah's depression by talking with him, but rather by providing him with food and rest.

I remember a time when I ended a Sunday extremely exhausted. Not only was I tired, but the tears flowed readily for no apparent reason. I reminded myself of the lessons learned from I Kings 19. I decided to get some extra rest (which I did) and to pray more than usual the next day. Prayer definitely does change things!

I Kings 19:11, 12, *"...And, behold, the LORD passed by, and a great and strong wind rent the mountains, and brake in pieces the rocks before the LORD; but the LORD was not in the wind: and after the wind an earthquake; but the LORD was not in the earthquake: And after the earthquake a fire; but the LORD was not in the fire: and after the fire a still small voice."* When Elijah began to pray, God began to show His strength to Elijah through a great and strong wind, then an earthquake, then a fire. But God did not show Himself to Elijah through any of these, but rather through a still, small voice. This reminds us of the importance of being still and quiet before God when we are depressed so that we might hear His voice.

Notice also how honest and specific Elijah was when he talked with God. I Kings 19:14, "*And he said, I have been very jealous for the LORD God of hosts: because the children of Israel have forsaken thy covenant, thrown down thine altars, and slain thy prophets with the sword; and I, even I only, am left; and they seek my life, to take it away.*"

We should be equally honest and specific in our conversations with God. We should tell Him our good and bad feelings; He knows all of them anyway. Elijah told God he was depressed over three things:

- The rejection of God and His commands among his peers. "*...I have been very jealous for the LORD God of hosts: because the children of Israel have forsaken thy covenant, thrown down thine altars, and slain thy prophets with the sword....*"
- Fear. "*...they seek my life, to take it away.*"
- Loneliness. "*...and I, even I only, am left....*"

These are common reasons for the depression of the servants of God and should be told to God specifically.

4. A friend is needed to fight depression. As soon as Elijah went through his bout of depression, God sent him a friend. I Kings 19: 19-21, "*So he departed thence, and found Elisha the son of Shaphat, who was plowing with twelve yoke of oxen before him, and he with the twelfth: and Elijah passed by him, and cast his mantle upon him. And he left the oxen, and ran after Elijah, and said, Let me, I pray thee, kiss my father and my mother, and then I will follow thee. And he said unto him, Go back again: for what have I done to thee? And he returned back from him, and took a yoke of oxen, and slew them, and boiled their flesh with the instruments of the oxen, and gave unto the people, and they did eat. Then he arose, and went after Elijah, and ministered unto him.*"

I am not sure it is wise to look for a friend. Friends are a gift from God. It seems like every time I have gone through a valley in my life, God has sent a friend. Perhaps if you are in depression right now, you might think of someone who is trying to minister to you. This may be the friend God is sending. Why not reach out to that friend and allow her to minister unto you?

One of the first symptoms of grief or depression in my own life is isolation—the desire to be left alone. When I went through the valley of depression in 1995, God sent a friend who ministered to me through her laughter. One of the steps I took to climb out of my depression was to begin calling this friend once a week to laugh with her for a while.

5. A support group is needed to fight depression. God's response to Elijah's feeling all alone was this: I Kings 19:18, *"Yet I have left me seven thousand in Israel, all the knees which have not bowed unto Baal, and every mouth which hath not kissed him."*

God reminded Elijah that 7,000 men in Israel believed like he did and had fought the same battle that Elijah had fought. This was the last thing God said to Elijah and the thing that seemed to get him back on his feet again.

I am not saying those who are depressed need to find a psychologist-led support group with whom to share their problems. I am saying that those who are depressed need to be faithful to their families and to their local churches for support.

All Christians should remember that the faces of other church members they see in church each week, though they may look serene, often mask another person who struggles with the same things with which they do. All people struggle all of the time. This includes people who sit on the platform of the church as well as in the audience. If we are unfaithful to our family and church in the good times, we will not have formed the support group we need for the bad times. Proverbs 30:27, *"The locusts have no king, yet go they forth all of them by bands."*

Proverbs 30:25-31 describes some of the members of the animal kingdom who possess a certain tenacity and the reasons why they do. The locusts multiply with tenacity, not because they have a king, but because they go forth in groups. One way a Christian lady can experience tenacity in her life is by joining herself to the support group of the local church. We who are experiencing any amount of victory in our Christian lives ought to be there to support others who are depressed.

Sometimes I have felt stressed or overwhelmed by the responsibilities of being the pastor's wife of First Baptist Church of Hammond, Indiana. When these times come, I remind myself that I am not alone. Thousands of ladies all across America have husbands who preach behind fundamental pulpits. These men have not bowed their knee to the image of worldliness. Their wives fight the same battle I fight and believe like I do. I do not call them to tell them my problems, but somehow just thinking about them and knowing they are there brings me great comfort. I know that they struggle at times like I do. Just knowing they march on encourages me to march on.

I must be faithful to my fellow laborers—not tearing down their ministries—because I need them. And they need me. To those of you who are experiencing depression in your lives, I have been where you are. There is victory on the other side, and I am on the other side to help you.

Are you a lonely pastor's wife? You are not alone. Thousands fight with you. Though I do not fight beside you, I fight with you. If you need me, I will help you! The main lesson I have learned from posttrauma depression is that there is victory on the other side! Hold on to God until the victory is yours!

Depression

ONCE DID A BIBLE study on the subject of depression in the book of Psalms. Five Psalms stood out to me as dealing with the subject of depression. They are Psalms 32, 39, 57, 142, and 145.

In my John R. Rice Reference Bible, two verses from these Psalms contain words or phrases which Dr. Rice interprets in his margin notes to mean depression. Psalm 32:3, *"When I kept silence, my bones waxed old through my roaring all the day long."*

Psalm 145:14, *"The LORD upholdeth all that fall, and raiseth up all those that be bowed down."* Bowed down is listed as meaning "depressed."

Listed below are symptoms of depression that can be found in the abovementioned Psalms. Bear in mind that all of the following Bible verses were written by a man who had been depressed.

1. No vitality; feeling weak and old. Have you ever felt yourself so discouraged that you didn't feel like doing anything and you had little or no energy? Psalm 32:3, 4, *"When I kept silence, my bones waxed old through my roaring all the day long. For day and night thy hand was heavy upon me:* [The events God allowed were hard to bear.] *my moisture is turned into the drought of summer. Selah."*

2. Inability to speak. A truly depressed person wants to be alone and has difficulty speaking or knowing what to say, even in prayer. Psalm 39:2, 9, *"I was dumb with silence, I held my peace, even from good; and my sorrow was stirred....I was dumb, I opened not my mouth; because thou didst it."*

3. Feeling alone. Many reasons arise for one's feeling depressed: grief over the death of a loved one, illness, change, church splits or battles, family strife, the loss of a friend or a position. Every depressed person comes to the point when he realizes no one can understand him or completely pull him out of his depression, except for God. Depression is a battle that is fought alone. Psalm 142:4, "*I looked on my right hand, and beheld, but there was no man that would know me: refuge failed me; no man cared for my soul.*"

4. Feeling overwhelmed. Psalm 142:3, "*When my spirit was overwhelmed within me, then thou knewest my path....*"

5. Feeling trapped. To the depressed person, their reality becomes a prison from which they cannot escape. Psalm 142:7, "*Bring my soul out of prison....*"

The Cure

The following are some cures given in the book of Psalms for the depressed person.

1. Confess your sin. Psalm 32:5, "*I acknowledged my sin unto thee, and mine iniquity have I not hid....*" I am not saying that sin is always the reason why a person is depressed. Depression does not always mean one is not right with God. However, I find that it is best to approach every problem as both practical and spiritual. I always want to be sure a clear line exists between God and me. For this reason, I confess my sins several times each day. I know there have been times I have been discouraged when God pointed out to me a sin that had a part in it.

2. Pray. Psalm 32:6, "*For this shall every one that is godly pray unto thee in a time when thou mayest be found....*" (Also see Psalm 39:3; 57:2; and 142:1, 2.) Tell God exactly how you are feeling. One of my strengths is that I am able to talk honestly with God. I tell Him all my feelings whether they are anger, jealousy, frustration, depression and so forth. Be thorough with God.

Many Christians say prayer is too trite of an answer. They would rather pop a pill in their mouth and have their depression disappear almost magically. God often seems to want us to pray it through until we gradually learn the lessons we need to learn. Lessons learned in haste are seldom really learned.

I once knew a lady who was depressed for a long period of time. She finally committed herself to a long season of prayer and fasting. Her depression left and never returned. *"I cried unto the LORD with my voice; with my voice unto the LORD did I make my supplication. I poured out my complaint before him; I shewed before him my trouble."* (Psalm 142:1, 2)

3. Hope in God. The Devil's two greatest lies to the depressed are these:

- You are crazy!
- You will never come out of this!

Recognize these as lies and never lose your hope. Psalm 39:7, *"And now, LORD, what wait I for? My hope is in thee."*

4. Trust the Lord. Again, this is one of those statements that seem trite to the average Christian. We want a magic potion instead. But magic potions often come from the Devil with more damaging side effects. Trust is not a feeling of confidence. The depressed person has little or no confidence. Trust is praying every day even when you feel miserable five minutes after getting off your knees.

It is saying to God, "I don't know what You are doing, but I will run to You and not from You, even if the pain never goes away." Psalm 32:10, *"Many sorrows shall be to the wicked, but he that trusteth in the LORD, mercy shall compass him about."*

5. Keep your mouth shut. The depressed person must come to the time where he realizes that no one else can help him, not even his spouse. Depression is like a river. Your Christian loved ones can walk up to the bank with you, but they cannot swim the river with you. It is okay to talk to your spouse; everyone needs someone with whom to talk, but rambling on and on often only postpones healing. Also, it is good to realize that depression does not give us a right to say whatever hurtful thing we want to say. Psalm 39:1, "*I said, I will take heed to my ways, that I sin not with my tongue: I will keep my mouth with a bridle, while the wicked is before me.*"

6. Fix your heart on praise. A depressed person doesn't want to hear about praising. The depressed person has forgotten how to praise. Something has happened, maybe many somethings which have broken the trust and the praise of the depressed person. A depressed person must teach herself to praise again, just like a first grader would learn to read. She must write down her praise, speak her praise out loud, play praise music, and sing praise music. She must occupy her negative mind with so much praise that the Devil's attacks cannot penetrate. She will get better at it in time, but praise will not chase away the depression all at once.

All Christians must fix their thoughts around praise 24/7. Otherwise, I think we will all eventually find something about which to be depressed. Psalm 57:7, "*My heart is fixed, O God, my heart is fixed: I will sing and give praise.*" The Bible tells us to fix upon only two things: trust and praise.

What God Will Do for the Depressed

1. **God will be a hiding place for the depressed.** Psalm 32:7, *"Thou art my hiding place...."* During a time of depression, God became my favorite retreat. I have never lost the joy of the glory of His presence.

2. God will give you a song. Psalm 32:7 continues, *"...thou shalt compass me about with songs of deliverance."* During a time of depression, I played a song recorded by the Marshall family over and over.

> *Y*ou are my hiding place
> You always fill my heart with songs of deliverance
> Whenever I am afraid,
> I will trust in You.
> I will trust in You.
> Let the weak say,
> "I am strong in the strength of the Lord."

During my lowest of times, I would play this song over and over. Other songs such as "Rejoice in the Lord," written by Ron Hamilton, were a great help, but "You Are My Hiding Place" was my song from the Lord in the night. I love to hear this song, and I am grateful to the Marshall family for recording it.

3. God will give you counsel and show you the way out. Psalm 32:8, "*I will instruct thee and teach thee in the way which thou shalt go....*" God did show me the way out of my depression. He also showed me through my depression how to handle much more difficult things which were to come. I have no doubt, looking back, that God was right there achieving His plan in my life during those dark days that were so hard for me to understand.

4. God will watch over you. Psalm 32:8 continues, "*...I will guide thee with mine eye.*" If you are depressed, don't believe the Devil when he says, "God has left you." This is a lie! God's eyes are upon you like never before.

5. God will have mercy. Psalm 32:10, "*Many sorrows shall be to the wicked: but he that trusteth in the LORD, mercy shall compass him about.*" This verse was written by David, so it is not saying that only the wicked will have sorrow. It is saying that those who trust the Lord in their sorrow will be surrounded by God's mercy. Again, trusting the Lord is not having a feeling of strong confidence. It is running to, and not from, the Lord even when you don't understand what He is doing.

The depressed person becomes so impatient with himself that he believes God must be angry at him and ready to strike him dead. In reality, God surrounds the depressed person with His mercy. Looking back on my own season of depression, I now see how God was infinitely patient. He even covered for me when it seemed that the whole world could see I was struggling.

6. God will hear. Psalm 145:18, "*The LORD is nigh unto all them that call upon him, to all that call upon him in truth.*" The depressed person feels his prayers bounce off the ceiling. That is only a feeling and not the truth. Every cry we make enters into the ears of Jehovah God.

7. God will raise you up. Psalm 145:14, "*The LORD upholdeth all that fall, and raiseth up all those that be bowed down.*" Again, those Bible words *bowed down* mean "depressed."

Notice that this verse does not say that God can heal some people's depression. It says that He can heal **all** of the people's depression. I can testify personally to this fact. God healed my depression.

8. God will give you joy. Psalm 32:11, *"Be glad in the LORD, and rejoice, ye righteous: and shout for joy, all ye that are upright in heart."*

Psalm 142:7, *"…the righteous shall compass me about; for thou shalt deal bountifully with me."*

God eventually brings what every depressed person longs for—joy! Joy on the other side of sorrow is different somehow. It is more mellow and yet it is deeper. It finds satisfaction in every simple thing.

The righteous often surround the person who has come out of depression God's way because that person has developed a lasting joy that they want to copy. The formerly depressed person has something to say because he has completed a journey where he has come to know more about true joy and about God.

To a person who has come out of depression, however, life is no longer about obtaining joy; life is about knowing and exalting God. Psalm 57:11, *"Be thou exalted, O God, above the heavens: let thy glory be above all the earth."*

Living on the Edge

My HUSBAND AND I RECENTLY returned from a wonderful vacation to the Acadia National Park in Maine. We spent two of our days together hiking in the park. Hiking is one of our family's favorite vacation activities. We stopped at the park information center to get some guidance about the best hiking trails. It must have humored the guide who helped us when she asked, "What type of trail are you looking for?" and my husband and I both answered at the same time. In the exact same second that he said "strenuous," I said "easy." In a marriage, sometimes compromise is good, and the guide pointed us to a "moderate" hiking trail.

On the way to the trail, we found a map. The map pointed one way to the moderate trail my husband and I had chosen and another way to a strenuous trail. "I think the moderate trail goes this way," my husband stated as he pointed. It looked to me like the map said that was the way to the strenuous trail, but I decided to follow my husband.

In a matter of 30 minutes, I found myself placing my feet on some very narrow bars and climbing straight up the side of a high and steep mountain. My husband had led me to the beehive trail which was marked "strenuous—high cliffs and narrow ledges, not recommended for children" (or me). A couple of times, I just stopped for a few seconds and panicked, but I continued on because I truly do love to hike with my husband. When we finished our hike, we sat on a ledge and pulled out our thermos of coffee. (You didn't expect me to hike without coffee, did you?) As we drank, we saw from our high vantage point a magnificent panoramic view of much of Acadia National Park. I was glad I had followed my husband on this strenuous trail.

On another hike my husband and I found a ledge where we could sit and drink our coffee. It was a stormy day, and as we sipped, we watched down the steep drop below us and saw ominous waves crashing over the rocky islands beneath. "Do you ever think about jumping when you get to a place like this?" he asked.

"No," I emphatically replied.

"I do," he said. (I will never feel the same watching him stand on the edge of our church platform again!)

Though I didn't think about jumping, I did think to myself about how much I enjoy watching danger—especially when I know it can't get to me. I thrilled at the sight of the deep and powerful waters below, realizing if I leaned just a little bit too much in the wrong direction, I would be swallowed up by the powerful waves. There I sat in my sweatshirt, pony tail, and baseball cap (pink, of course), with my husband, and as I sat, I thought, "This is so like our lives as pastor and pastor's wife of First Baptist Church of Hammond. We are always living on the edge. Sometimes it seems like one small move in the wrong direction, and we will be swallowed by the depth and power of the responsibility." I was enveloped, not by waves, but by a very familiar insecure feeling.

The greatest danger to the pastor's wife is not rocky ledges or ocean waves. The greatest danger to a pastor's wife is the danger of insecurity.

Most of my security as a child was found in my relationship with my father. I was afraid of tornadoes, and when a tornado warning was issued, I drove my mother crazy with fear. But when my dad arrived home, all fear of a tornado ceased. I suppose I realized even then that my dad could not take away the tornado or stop it in its path, but my dad was my security. If he was present, everything would be all right—somehow, someway.

When I married my husband in 1979, I saw very little of my dad for the first few years. I became frustrated with his busy schedule. I didn't realize it then, but I realize now that Dad became "extra busy" on purpose. He wanted me to find my security in my new husband, and that is what I did. The very same "everything-will-be-all-right" feeling that I used to associate with my father's presence is now associated with my husband's presence. My father moved out of the way, and my husband took his place.

One month after my father died in 2001, my husband became pastor of what is technically called a megachurch, the First Baptist Church of Hammond, Indiana. As I grieved the loss of my father, I began to share my husband in a new way with a host of people. As his wife, there is a part of my husband that belongs only to me, but as a pastor, there is a part of him that belongs to me only if there is no emergency or if no one dies. Not long after my husband's pastorate began, an old familiar feeling tried to settle in. It was the feeling of insecurity—sort of like one long tornado warning. Just like with my father years before, I could no longer find all of my security in my husband, and yet this time it was different—because no one else should, could, or would take his place.

Hebrews 4:15 says, *"For we have not an high priest which cannot be touched with the feeling of our infirmities...."* This verse teaches us that Jesus does not just know the weakness of insecurity, but He can feel the feelings of insecurity. Jesus can feel the weakness of the insecure.

He is touched by the feeling of:

- a forced smile
- being set apart from a crowd, feeling like you don't fit in
- trying to think of someone to talk to about your fears and realizing there is no one

- an intense loneliness
- breaking down and telling someone your fears, walking away, and knowing that person does not understand
- feeling judged by people you don't even know
- feeling inadequate, like you let a host of people down

Jesus is touched by the feeling of insecurity—an intense pain that goes unnoticed because it carries no accompanying illness.

Insecurity is a feeling that all human beings carry at times, and because I am somewhat partial to pastors' wives, I, in particular, think of the insecurities that they carry.

The journey to true security is an exciting adventure, kind of like a strenuous, uphill climb. And though I don't believe I have made it to the top, the view is more and more panoramic as I climb; it just keeps getting prettier and prettier.

Some people start the journey early. An abusive parent, a divorce, rejection, a handicap, etc. can start people on this journey early—sometimes before they are ready to start it. I was a lucky one. By the time I started my journey, I had known years of the security of loving parents, a godly husband, and a happy family. Yet still I had to begin my ascent to true security. You see, true security does not even come from loving parents, a godly husband, or a happy family. Sooner or later, we all must learn this—or reject this.

True security comes solely from Who God is! This sounds like a big disappointment until we discover just Who He really is. And Who is God? God is unequivocally and undisputably FAITHFUL!

Jesus is as faithful to you as He has been to bring a sunrise every morning and a sunset each evening. He is as faithful to you as He is to bring the four seasons—spring, summer, fall, and winter. He is as faithful to you as the rainbow after the rain. He is as faithful to you as the ebb and tide and the constant roar of the mighty ocean.

If you could see with spiritual eyes during your insecure moments, you would see Jesus, not just standing beside you, but with His arms wrapped tightly around you, hearing your every word and going to work on your every request, and best of all, feeling those strange feelings that no even knows are there. He feels the feelings that you cannot even understand yourself. Jesus always answers our feelings and our prayers—maybe not always in the way we wanted, but always in the way that is best for us— always in the faithful way!

So to you readers and to you pastors' wives in particular, the next time you have that old familiar feeling of insecurity, picture yourself on the ragged edge of a steep cliff with angry ocean waves straight beneath you. Then picture the strongest arms you can imagine holding you more tightly than you have ever been held. Those arms are stronger than the ocean. Look up and see the kindest face you have ever seen and realize that you never, never, never have to be insecure.

Oh, and one more thing—if you realized that Jesus was your true security, how high would you be willing to climb for Him? I encourage you to keep climbing—the panoramic view (or the big picture of your life) will be truly beautiful and worth the climb!

Pastor's wife, I know that the trail your husband has chosen can be a strenuous one, but I encourage you to keep following him. It is worth it to spend your life living on the edge!

Step 6

Know Where
to
Find Security!

Security

*M*ORE THAN ONCE SINCE my dad has been in Heaven, I have found a note or an outline that has helped me as I was studying for a particular article. He always did like to have his hand in everything; sometimes it seems like he still has his hand in some things! I had been planning to write about insecure people when I came across the following outline in my father's Bible.

Survey—"What do you want most?"

1. Security
2. Happiness
3. Prosperity

I believe that about 99% of people are insecure. That statistic means that in any given situation, when we are worried about what others think about us, they are probably thinking about themselves. Is there not any way we can leave our own world and think about others? Are we all destined to be insecure the rest of our lives, or can we live above this?

Hebrews 4:9 says, *"There remaineth therefore a rest to the people of God."* My John R. Rice Reference Bible interprets the word *rest* to mean either "security" or "peace," and I believe that both interpretations are closely related. So, Hebrews 4:9 tells us that security is available to the people of God. How do we find that rest? How do we find security in a world where the majority of people seem almost consumed with insecurity?

1. Unbelief hinders us from being secure. Hebrews 4:5, 6 says, *"And in this place again, If they shall enter into my rest. Seeing* *therefore it remaineth that some must enter therein, and they to whom it was first preached entered not in because of unbelief.*"The more our faith is strengthened, the more secure we will be.

2. Listening to the Word of God, whether it be through preaching or through direct reading of the Bible, strengthens our faith and gives us rest. Hebrews 4:7, "*...To day if ye will hear his voice, harden not your hearts.*" In 2004 my husband preached an awesome sermon (totally biased judgment) where he taught that obedience strengthens our faith. As I get older, and as I see the world changing for the worse, I long to have more faith. I told the Lord at that time that if it is obedience which strengthens my faith, I want to "obey more in '04."

When we stick our neck out (like building an ark when it has never rained), do something God asks (something we don't want to do), and then see God come through, our faith is strengthened. And faith brings rest—security and peace of mind.

3. Security comes from ceasing from our own works. Hebrews 4:10, "*For he that is entered into his rest, he also hath ceased from his own works, as God did from his.*" I know that there is no work I have to do to obtain salvation. Jesus has done it all. In receiving Him as my Saviour, I have rest concerning my eternity. On this earth, security is obtained by ceasing from my own works, also. To be honest, I believe my level of security has grown through the years. Why? I spend time in Bible reading and prayer every day. While doing so, I ask God to live His life through me. Daily I pray something like this,

Dear God,

Come and be through me today all that You would have me to be as You would have me to be it.

In other words, God, through me, is being the wife, the mother, the teacher, the worker, and so forth that He wants me to be.

Knowing He is in charge gives me the confidence I need to stand before 250 students each week and teach them about the Christian life. I am secure that God is doing the work and that the work will be competent and useful to His kingdom. I do not have to compare myself with others, think about my weaknesses, or become jealous when God uses some other woman in a great way. I'm not doing the work anyway. I have ceased from trying to do a work on my own, and God is doing through me whatever He wants done through my particular life. When I fail, there doesn't need to be a lot of self-condemnation or self-introspection. I just need to ask a couple of simple questions such as: 1) Have I been disobedient? or 2) Have I walked with God as I should?

Mostly, I just need to ask God's forgiveness and quickly start again with God in control of my works. I know I am flesh—it's no big deal. Let's just try again! God will get it right if I continue to cling to Him!

4. Security comes from being obedient in the labor God asks me to do with the right motive. Hebrews 4:11, 12 *"Let us labour therefore to enter into that rest, lest any man fall after the same example of unbelief. For the word of God is quick, and powerful,…and is a discerner of the thoughts and intents of the heart."* It seems paradoxical. Security comes from ceasing from your own work in verse ten. In verse eleven, security comes from laboring. The motive is the key. If I am laboring in the work of God to impress myself or others with my own works, I will never have peace. I will live my life exhausted and insecure.

If I am laboring to be obedient to the unique task God asks me to do, if I am trusting that the works are of His grace and ability, and not my own, I can work hard, accomplish a lot and still be at rest and secure.

Yet I must labor; I must do my part. God will decide how many souls I win this week. That is His work. But I must labor by knocking on some doors and sharing the plan of salvation. God will move the hearts of the college girls I teach, but I must obey Him by preparing and standing before the class to teach the material.

5. Security comes from knowing that God knows all of our imperfections, and He wants to use us anyway. Hebrews 4:13, "*Neither is there any creature that is not manifest in his sight: but all things are naked and opened unto the eyes of him with whom we have to do.*" In other words, we don't have to get all uptight about our strengths or our weaknesses because the One for Whom we're working knows exactly with whom He's dealing. Our works do not impress Him.

When we understand that God is our fellow laborer—our Productivity Manager—and He knows exactly how insufficient we are—it makes our job seem easier and a lot more restful!

6. Security comes from knowing that God is merciful and gracious, and He wants to help us to help others in their time of need. Hebrews 4:14, 15, 16, "*Seeing then that we have a great high priest, that is passed into the heavens, Jesus the Son of God, let us hold fast our profession. For we have not an high priest which cannot be touched with the feeling of our infirmities; but was in all points tempted like as we are, yet without sin. Let us therefore come boldly unto the throne of grace, that we may obtain mercy, and find grace to help in time of need.*" Ahhhh! I feel a lot more secure just reading those verses!

The members of First Baptist Church of Hammond, Indiana, have a pastor's wife who has nothing to offer them. I am young and inexperienced, and even worse than that, I am human. But God wants to help me to help the people of our church as their pastor's wife. With Him, I have everything to offer the people whom I serve, as I have heard more than one preacher say, "Work (or obey) as if it all depended on you. Pray (and believe) as if it all depended on God."

The Christian who truly grasps those two thoughts on a step-by-step basis can be at rest, have peace of mind, and be secure.

The Christian who grasps these thoughts can leave his own world of "What are other people thinking about me?" and can enter the world of others.

When the Insecure Become Secure

*I*N THE SECTION ON "KNOW Your Enemy," I wrote about the flesh, one of the three enemies of the Christian. I described the flesh as being what causes us to desire to impress others. As a Christian, our aim should be to "bless and not impress." When we interact within our relationships with a desire to impress others, our mind is on our self and not on those we should be trying to help. When we are self-centered or self-focused in any relationship, that relationship will struggle and suffer harm.

I was reading Psalm 16:8, 9 in my devotions, and the Lord brought to my attention a lesson on the flesh. *"I have set the LORD always before me: because he is at my right hand, I shall not be moved. Therefore my heart is glad, and my glory rejoiceth: my flesh also shall rest in hope."* In the margin of my John R. Rice Reference Bible, the word *rest* was said to mean "be secure."

It is insecurity that causes us to be fleshly in our approach to people. Insecurity is a great problem with women. Whenever I see the word "secure" in my studies, I take great notice. I want to help women to get along with each other better. Therefore, I must learn how to help women to feel secure. What is it in Psalm 16 that causes the psalmist David to feel secure and hopeful?

1. Security comes from *"setting the Lord always before me."* In Psalm 16 David speaks of his trust in the Lord (v. 1) and how the Lord is his portion (all he wants, v. 5), but I think all of David's thoughts about the Lord in this Psalm can be concluded and summarized in one thought: "I have set the Lord always before me."

One of the most simple and helpful thoughts I ever read on carnal versus spiritual thinking is this:

- To be carnally minded is to think about self.
- To be spiritually minded is to think about God.

To be spiritually minded, one must set God always before himself. This is why I strive to meet with God first thing every morning through the Bible and prayer. I also strive to reacquaint myself with Him throughout each day, to look for Him, and to notice with praise every big and little thing He does to show Himself to me.

2. Security comes from stability. David said that because he had set the Lord always before him, he would not be moved. People who are consumed with self are constantly changing. They tend to frequently change where they live. They often change churches and positions. There is not a position large enough or with enough notoriety to satisfy the flesh. They change their thoughts about God's will and their standards according to what seems to impress the type of people who currently surround them.

People who have their thoughts centered on God are easily led by God as stated in Psalm 16:11, *"Thou wilt shew me the path of life...."* They are contented with their house, their area, their church, and their position. God is the guide Who preserves them in His will. God is their never-changing measuring stick for their standards.

At this writing, I have lived in the same house for 24 years, and I love it. I have attended the same church for all of my 47 years, and I love it. Hold on to your seat—I believe the most beautiful area in which to live is in Northwest Indiana—and no, I am not lying! God's ways of showing Himself are just as beautiful in my little town as they are anywhere else in the universe!

I was very happy as the wife of the vice president of Hyles-Anderson College. When God made it clear that my husband was to become pastor of First Baptist Church of Hammond, I was happy, but for a few months I grieved the loss of contact with the college students. They had been our ministry, and we dearly loved them.

I believe that I have been preserved in God's will for all of my life. Why? Because I am a great person? No! I am a weak person who is beset with dying flesh. Left to myself, I am completely self-ish and unstable, but I have a great God, and if I set Him ALWAYS before me, I am able to stay in God's will and to prop-erly love others.

3. Security comes from true joy. When a person sets the Lord always before him, the end result is stability in God's will. The combination of God-centered thoughts and doing God's will brings contentment and true joy. Psalm 16:8, 9 shows God's plan for true security.

- *"I have set the* LORD *always before me...."* (God-cen-tered thoughts)
- *"...because he is at my right hand, I shall not be moved."* (Stability in God's will)
- *"Therefore my heart is glad, and my glory rejoiceth."* (True joy) [*Therefore* means "because of what came before."]
- *"...my flesh also shall rest* ["be secure"] *in hope."*

Do you lack hope about your future? Do you feel that your house or wardrobe is not good enough? Are you discontented with where God has placed you or the position He has given you? Do you feel inadequate to help others? Are you jealous of what is the lot of someone else? All of these thoughts bring us to the point where we hurt people instead of helping them, even those we feel we love the most.

What is the answer? Day by day spend your time thinking

about God. May I recommend that you read and study the chapter entitled "Distracted—A Lesson on Mary and Martha" in my book *A Meek and Quiet Spirit*?

I wish that God was in all of my thoughts, but I am learning to think of Him more and more. What a wonderful God He is! I am living proof that God can take the "least of these" and use her to help others. Those who have every reason to be insecure can become secure by setting the Lord always before them.

What Gives Me Confidence

"And hereby we know that we are of the TRUTH, and shall ASSURE our hearts before him. For if our heart condemn us, God is greater than our heart, and knoweth all things. Beloved, if our heart CONDEMN us not, then have we CONFIDENCE toward God. And whatsoever we ask, we receive of him, because we keep his commandments, and do those things that are pleasing in sight. And this is his commandment, That we should believe on the name of his Son Jesus Christ, and LOVE one another, as he gave us commandment." (I John 3:19-23)

Being confident and self-assured is a big issue with most ladies. As I have already stated, I believe that 99% of people are insecure, and I have not met the person who isn't. Those who say they are not are probably just too insecure to admit it! The book of I John has an oft-repeated theme of "confidence" and "assurance." This book teaches how to have assurance of salvation (I John 5:13) as well as addressing other areas of assurance. When reading I John 3:19-23 recently, those words "confidence" and "assurance" in this passage jumped out at me once more.

I do not always feel confident as the pastor's wife of the First Baptist Church of Hammond, Indiana. I have a personal vision of what a pastor's wife should look like. My predecessor, who is also my mother, looks to me like a pastor's wife. She lights up a room with her beauty. I, on the other hand, do not! I would love it if God would have made me to look like my mother. (It seems if He wanted me to follow in her footsteps, He could have made me look like her!)

Instead, I look like my father, who was a wonderful pastor before he went to Heaven, but he would have made a lousy pastor's wife, in looks anyway! This is just one of the reasons that I sometimes lack the assurance I need as a pastor's wife.

It is easy for a woman to lack confidence as a soul winner, as a wife, as a mother, and in many other areas. To succeed as a pastor's wife or in any of these other areas, one must have confidence, however. To be honest with you, as long as I focus on God and His Word, I have complete confidence that I can do and be whatever God wants for me to do and be. It is only my flesh that gets in the way occasionally. Allow me to share with you a confidence killer, and then I will share how God gives me my confidence. The greatest confidence killer is to have a heart that feels condemned before God! Our heart may feel condemned because we are unable to comprehend what a forgiving and loving God we have.

I used to be a very self-condemning person. Before my husband and I were married, in fact after just a few dates, he saw that need in my life. He took out his Bible and became the first guy I had ever dated who read the Bible to me. He ministered to my need with Psalm 78:38, 39, which says, *"But he, being full of compassion, forgave their iniquity, and destroyed them not: yea, many a time turned he his anger away, and did not stir up all his wrath. For he remembered that they were but flesh; a wind that passeth away, and cometh not again."*

It is good to fear God; I'm glad that I learned to fear Him. But it is not good to live your life thinking God is angry at you and ready to "bring down the hammer" for every mistake you make. Some of us feel condemned in our hearts before God because we are not right with Him. I John 3:19-23 gives us reasons that our heart might be condemned before God.

1. **Not being saved will cause our heart to condemn us before God.** The unsaved person lacks assurance and confidence about eternity and, therefore, about all of life.

2. **A lack of obedience will cause our heart to condemn us before God.** Even a saved person can lack assurance of salvation and confidence in his life if he is disobedient to God. Disobedience does not make a person lose his salvation, but it can cause him to lose his assurance of salvation. Disobedience will make a person feel condemned in his heart to God, and it will also cause him to lack confidence.

3. **A lack of prayer will cause our heart to condemn us before God.** *"And whatsoever we ask, we receive of him, because we keep his commandments, and do those things that are pleasing in his sight."* (I John 3:22) I strongly believe one of the main things that gives me the confidence to be a pastor's wife and to do the things that I do is my relationship with the Bible and prayer. My knowledge of the Bible gives me confidence that I have something to offer my husband and the members of First Baptist Church.

When I am prayed up over the things that are on my heart and concern me, I am full of confidence. If I neglect my time in prayer, my heart condemns me before God and destroys my confidence.

My husband has graciously provided an office for me at First Baptist Church of Hammond. No, I am not the co-pastor; I am just the wife of the pastor. Yet, because I wait an average of an hour and a half after each evening service, my husband has provided me with a comfortable office where I can counsel and relax. Hardly a service goes by that I do not spend some time alone in that office before the service begging God, not only to bless the service and my husband, but also to be through me what the people of our church need me to be and what God and my husband want me to be.

On Sunday mornings I spend a great deal of time begging God

alone in my office. Why? Because without Jesus, I have nothing to offer as a pastor's wife. Without prayer, I really don't have any confidence to do anything.

Someone recently said to me, "You appear so confident." I had to chuckle to myself and also praise the Lord. I AM so confident, as long as I am walking so close to the Lord.

4. A lack of love will cause our heart to condemn us before God. It is no coincidence that these verses which teach so much about confidence and assurance also mention loving one another.

I am not a Bible scholar, but if I had to describe the greatest themes of the book of I John, I would say they are "confidence," "assurance," and "love." We cannot walk in true confidence unless we love people. We cannot be right with God unless we are right with people. If we are not right with others, our heart will condemn us before God, and our confidence will be shot!

I used to be embarrassed and self-conscious to be introduced as Dr. Jack Hyles' daughter. I have also struggled with being introduced as the wife of Dr. Jack Schaap. As I have learned and relearned not to think about myself, but rather to think about loving the people to whom I am talking, my assurance and confidence have replaced the embarrassment.

My dad used to say he worried about some new pastor's taking his place and not loving the members of First Baptist like a pastor of 41 years would. I never fully realized that my husband would be the next pastor, but I remember striving to love our church people as my parents did when I was just the pastor's daughter.

I can definitely verify that our new pastor loves his church members. These church members are easy for me to love; I grew up with many of them. Yet I love the brand new members too and even the former members who have left our church. Why? Because God commands me to love them. I emphasize love in my heart, and that love gives me the confidence and the assurance that I have something to offer each member of our church.

The Love Factor

Allow me to break down the love factor from I John 3:19-23 into points.

1. *A person who hurts, criticizes, condemns and competes with people does so because of lack of confidence.* He feels that tearing someone else down will make him feel better about himself.

2. *A person who hurts people will feel condemned in his heart before God.* This person may not admit it, but in his heart he knows he is wrong and feels condemned.

3. *Feeling condemned in his heart before God destroys a person's confidence.* A vicious cycle will continue as a person hurts more and more people and continuously destroys his already shattered confidence.

4. *Confidence will be restored and enhanced as truth and love replace criticism and hurt in a person's life.* I know that I have hurt many people in my life. I have not always handled every person properly, even since becoming the editor of *Christian Womanhood*. But when I have hurt a person, I have confessed it honestly before God. I have also apologized to every person when I thought an apology was due. I have never intentionally attacked anyone, nor do I ever plan to do so. God is big enough to do this for me if needs be. There is not a person to whom I will not speak. There are no grudges. There is no one whose hand I cannot shake and whom I cannot look in the eye.

I am not a great Christian; I struggle with fleshly sins like jealousy, selfishness, and greed as much as anyone, I suppose. But I believe my heart is right with God and with all of my fellow men. God has given me a love for all those who cross my path and a special love for our dear church members. It is His love, not mine.

My love is shallow and useless. His love is deep and enduring. And this love in my uncondemned (forgiven) heart is where my confidence comes from.

Let's not fail to love every one of God's children. For it is therein that we shall find the confidence to do and to be whatever God asks of us.

Step 7

Triumph
Over
Bitterness!

Handling Bitterness

I FEEL THAT I HAVE had about as happy a life as anyone can have; yet, I feel I know as well as anyone else what it is like to be hurt or to have a loved one hurt by another person. For most of my life, I have not struggled with the feeling of bitterness. I believe I can honestly say that there is not a person in my life whom I do not love. To be hurt by another and then to look in your heart and find love residing there is truly one of the greatest feelings in the world. Yet, in the last couple of years, I have found myself confronted with the awful feeling of bitterness.

I hesitate to admit bitterness, not because I am afraid to admit my flaws, but because my family has always been in such a public position. I am concerned that my readers will try to figure out toward whom I felt bitterness and will go unhelped. Bitterness often lands in some unsuspecting places; I assure you that no one knows against whom I found myself bitter, nor would I want anyone to know.

I have, however, learned some things about bitterness which I would like to share with you.

1. When you are bitter, you carry your wound with you. One morning I woke up with this awful feeling of bitterness. I immediately knew that such a feeling was wrong, and I wanted to make it go away right then! Whom could I call? What could I do? I felt very guilty about my feelings. Looking back, I think the guilt might have been even worse than the actual bitterness. I went to my husband for advice. Going to the right person for advice is a good start in dealing with bitterness. This should be one person and one person alone. My husband gave me my first step of direction in dealing with bitterness. He said, "Don't do anything until you know exactly what to do."

So, I decided to carry my bitterness with me, but I did leave the guilt and the impatience behind. This did make the load of my bitterness lighter.

2. Accept your wound. Many years ago, during one of our church's most difficult battles, I said the wedding vows to the Lord. I prayed: "I, Cindy Schaap, take Thee, Jesus Christ, to be my Lord and Saviour, to have and to hold from this day forward, for better or for worse, for richer or for poorer, in sickness and in health, to love, cherish, and obey...." I didn't say " 'till death do us part" because nothing will ever part us.

When I made that vow to the Lord, I was saying that I would always trust Him and walk with Him. I would always cherish Him as my Lord no matter what happened to me.

When bitterness cropped up in my life, I could almost instantly accept the fact that God had allowed my hurt to come to pass, and I accepted it as being from my Heavenly Father's hand.

Another part of accepting my wound was not trying to make my hurt go away. As soon as I looked squarely at the fact that my hurt might not leave me and that those who had hurt me may never stop trying to hurt me, added peace came to my heart.

3. Put medicine on your wound. When a person has a physical illness, we know to give him medicine and extra doses of vitamins. If a person has cancer, we give him chemotherapy. If a person has a cold, we may give him megadoses of Vitamin C.

A person suffering from a spiritual illness must apply a similar practice. The bitter person must apply to his wound megadoses of the Bible and prayer. Sometimes even good Christian people will admonish you to do something about your hurt and to do it right away (usually these are people who have not been asked). The more people push in these areas, the more time I set aside for myself to do nothing...but to seek the face of the Lord.

4. **Give your bitterness to the Lord every day.**
   - Confess to the Lord that you are bitter.
   - Admit to the Lord that your bitterness is your fault and not the fault of the person who hurt you.
   - Tell the Lord that you take full responsibility for your bitterness. Do not make excuses to the Lord.
   - Tell the Lord that you are sorry.
   - Ask the Lord to forgive you.
   - Ask the Lord to show you the way out of your bitterness.
   - Leave your bitterness with the Lord until the same time the next day.
   - If bitter thoughts come into your mind, ignore them.

I believe that one of the great secrets to the Christian life is to be completely honest with God. I don't know why this is so difficult because God knows all about us anyway. He knows that we have the power to resist sin, in spite of what others may do to us. When we are dishonest with God, we are really being dishonest with ourselves. We cannot grow in the Lord until we take full responsibility for our own sins.

5. **Don't try to figure out the offender who caused your wound.** Two verses helped me immensely in my journey out of bitterness. Proverbs 3:5, 6, *"Trust in the LORD with all thine heart; and lean not unto thine own understanding. In all thy ways acknowledge him, and he shall direct thy paths."*

When I am hurt, one of my greatest temptations is to try to figure out the offender. I think such thoughts as these: "If I could just find out why the person has hurt me," or "If I could just get the person to see it my way and to say, 'I'm sorry.' " To trust in God means that we don't have to understand why the person has hurt us. I don't understand why a father would sexually abuse his own child. The truth is that I don't want to understand; if I understood, I would be thinking like the offender.

People do not think alike. I think I am accurate in saying that no two people think alike. That is why we hurt each other in the first place. Sometimes when I have been hurt, I have felt sure that if I explained myself, the offender would see it my way, only to be shocked to find the person did not. I trust the Lord when I say, "I don't have to ever understand why a person has offended me." Understanding is not the issue; trust in God is the issue.

6. Take the first step of obedience. This is where trusting the Lord comes in handy! Daily we acknowledge Him. "Lord, show me what to do about my bitterness." Then we wait for His direction.

Sometimes we have people in our lives whose lifestyles are truly evil. The Lord may direct us to pray for and to love that person from afar. God's direction may prompt us to stay away from that person.

Oftentimes a day will come when the Lord directs us to write a note or to make a phone call to a person who has offended us. Wait until you know what the Lord wants you to do, but do not wait until you want to do what He asks. That time may never come! It may be hard, but once the first step of obedience is taken, it is amazing how easy the next steps become. God's hand of blessing once again pours forth on the person who has repented of his bitterness! With bitterness in the past, the sky is bluer, the sun is brighter, and all of God's blessings seem sweeter!

7. If you have offended the one toward whom you have been bitter, say you are sorry! When people never admit that they are wrong or say that they are sorry, they quit growing spiritually. A person who is not growing spiritually is dying spiritually. If there is even a one percent chance that I am at fault, I want to say, "I'm sorry." Remember, if a person refuses to apologize, he leaves the offended one with nothing to forgive.

8. Forgive! I am not an advocate of the "forgive-and-forget" philosophy. I don't believe a person ever forgets the hurts he experiences at the hands of others. A child who has been abused will never forget. She can, however, forgive. She can also keep her mind busy thinking on positive and spiritual things so that she does not allow herself to think about the past.

9. Treat the person as if he never offended you. I used to wonder how a person could practice the verse which says "...*love covereth all sins.*" (Proverbs 10:12) Now that I am older, I understand that is the only way to forgive.

Bitterness occurs when a person is hurt in such a way or at such a time that he really cannot understand why the offense was allowed to take place. It is impossible to rationalize bitterness away. The only way to forgive is not to forget—but rather to decide to act like the offense never happened. Some people get bitter, and they spend the rest of their lives treating a person like a criminal or like an outcast. Again, there may be a time when we must love a person from afar. But it is possible to forgive those who have offended us.

I used to find it difficult to cry when thinking about Jesus' death on the Cross. Since my journey through bitterness, I rarely sing about the Crucifixion without tears filling my eyes. I want to forgive like Christ did, not because it is the **easy** way, but because it is the **only** way. Christ's way is the only way out of our bitterness.

Christ said to those who hurt Him, "I forgive you. I don't think you really know what you are doing. [We don't think like He does.] Still, I will bear the responsibility for your sin, and I love you...just...as...if...you...had...never...sinned." No wonder the song writer wrote, "Oh, what a Saviour is mine!" He is a Saviour Who can forgive all of the perversion and violence in this world, and He is the Saviour Who can forgive the ugly, awful sin of bitterness! Jesus knows the way out of your bitterness!

The Odious Woman

$\mathscr{P}$ROVERBS 30:21-23 TELLS US that there are four things that the earth cannot bear.

1. "…*a servant when he reigneth…*"
2. "…*a fool when he is filled with meat.*"
3. "…*an odious woman when she is married…*"
4. "…*an handmaid that is heir to her mistress.*"

What in the world is an *odious* woman? At first glance, it seems it may be a woman who smells bad. That is indeed hard to bear, but that is not what an odious woman is.

I looked up the words "odious woman" and discovered them to mean "a woman who was unloved in her previous life and, therefore, sour and ill-tempered in her marriage." An odious woman is not a woman who smells bad, but a woman who has a stinking attitude. Yet this woman has a very good reason for her stinking attitude. She was unloved in the life that she lived before she was married. How awful to feel unloved!

Often, those who counsel come across a couple who have ugly and complicated problems in their marriage. Just as often, it seems that those problems are traced back to a negative experience in their childhood—the life that they lived previous to their marriage. Frequently, that negative experience involves rejection from a mother or a father.

I wish that I could do something to help our readers who were unloved in their previous lives to keep from carrying a stinking attitude into their future lives and into their marriages. This chapter is written to help those who have been rejected not only by their parents, but also by siblings. It is written to help those who are divorced—those whose previous life involved being unloved by a husband or a wife.

1. Don't become bitter at your family. Accept the fact that you felt rejected by a family member. Take a deep breath and say to God, "I accept the fact that I felt unloved by ___." (You fill in the blank.) Realize that person who has hurt you was probably doing the best he knew how. If you had parents who rejected you, they probably had a parent who rejected them. They related to you the only way they knew how. Why don't you stop that cycle of rejection with your own husband and children? God can help you to do that! Thank God for the rejection you have felt. God can use it to work good in your life as soon as you thank Him for it.

I Thessalonians 5:18, *"In every thing give thanks: for this is the will of God in Christ Jesus concerning you."*

Also, realize that your loved ones may have felt love in their heart for you; they may have even felt they were expressing it properly. They just didn't know how to take it from their heart into their words and actions in such a way that you could understand it. Forgive them for their error by never seeking revenge, but by seeking to honor them in whatever way is appropriate and not harmful to you, your spouse, and your children.

Psalm 106:5 says, *"That I may see the good of thy chosen...."* Try to think only of what your loved one did that was good in your previous life. Try to focus on their good qualities. When bad qualities come to mind, tell yourself, "I'm not going there." (The Devil is the one who wants to take you there.)

Restore the relationships of the past with prayer and advice from your pastor and husband. If the relationship cannot be restored, don't live your life kicking yourself or anybody else about it. Don't live with regret!

2. Make it a lifelong adventure to learn how much God loves you. My husband teaches that there are several "satellites" that God uses to testify of His reality and of His love for us.

• *Creation.* Enjoy nature. When you see something you enjoy in nature, recognize it as a sign of God's love for you. Tell God you love Him and that you know He loves you. God uses all of nature to draw His people to Him. God says that His people are "His *portion.*" ["All He really wants"] Everything else that belongs to God is used to draw us to Him because God really loves us. Deuteronomy 32:9, "*For the LORD's portion is his people.…*"

• *The Bible.* Read the Bible daily. Memorize verses that tell how much God loves you. Do a Bible study on the love of God. There is no need to feel rejected. You are deeply loved by the best that there is!

• *The Local Church.* Be faithful to church and listen to your pastor as he preaches to you about the One Who will never reject you.

• *Other Christians.* Watch other Christians who know how to express love. Study their lives and their marriages. Read their books. Learn how to express love from them.

Though I have been dearly loved all of my life, I plan to study the love of God for the rest of my life. I know God is the only loved One Who is 100% faithful and that His love is fully satisfying.

3. Don't allow the relationships of the present to be hindered by hurtful relationships of the past. It is hard for those who have been rejected to believe that someone loves them. MAKE A COMMITMENT TO BELIEVE YOUR HUSBAND LOVES YOU! Accept the love of all of those among your family, friends, and co-workers.

It is also difficult for those who feel unloved to believe that the love they receive from their spouse won't go away. They are afraid of losing their love, even because of silly reasons like a small weight gain or an imperfection in their appearance.

The odious spouse may have a heart completely filled with deep love for others. Yet they may appear to be nothing but a crabby grouch (sour and ill-tempered) because fear prevents them from showing that love.

I often advise the lovelorn in this way: it is better to love someone and to treat him or her with kindness and to be rejected than to lose someone who loved you because you never took the dare of revealing your heart full of unconditional love to that person. Do not push people away because you were pushed away in your previous life. Accept the love that is available in many avenues of your life. You accept love by showing love through your words and your actions.

Though I hate divorce, I admire those who have gone on to love others after an unwanted divorce. They did not allow the rejection of one to cause them to reject others.

4. Quit searching for relationships you don't have. Enjoy the ones you do have. Though I hurt for the victims of divorce, I do not believe it is wise for a divorcee to live her life for only one thing—searching to be married again. The older you are, the less chance there is that you will find someone again.

Why spend your life pining over unrequited love? Why not leave your prayer request for a husband with God each morning and then fill your mind with the love you have from children, grandchildren, and friends throughout the rest of each day?

A famous preacher once said, "Wallow in the Word." That is a great idea, but I would like to add another, "Wallow in the love of God." Cozy up in the love of God every day like a fresh, fluffy goose-down comforter. Wrap it around you; it is your only foolproof method for finding love. But it is more than enough! With the love of God in your heart, you can meet rejection after rejection in your life and still influence the world—not as a crabby old lady who is sour, ill-tempered and, yes, odious—but as a woman who is full of love and acceptance for her husband, her family, and those around her.

What to Do When You Have Family Problems

AFTER RECEIVING AN UNUSUAL number of phone calls and letters asking me what to do regarding various family problems, I decided to study this very important subject. That study became a chapter for this book.

1. Realize God loves you! It is of extra importance to the person who has been hurt by a family problem to learn to find his (or her) love and security from God. One way that I "psyche" myself as a pastor's wife is this: I am constantly on the lookout for the love of God. Even though I have a wonderful family, the nature of my husband's and my ministry causes us to be confronted daily with a lot of hurts. Finding my strength and joy in the love of God gives me a supply that does not dwindle even during the most hurtful days.

As the editor of the *Christian Womanhood* magazine, I periodically mention in articles that I write how I keep a journal of the things that God does each day to show me He loves me. Every day I ask God to show Himself to me, and then I write down at least one way that He does.

One Sunday afternoon I looked in the refrigerator and saw some containers of applesauce. I am not a great fan of applesauce, but it sounded very good to me at that moment. I needed to leave for choir, so instead of eating it, I made a mental note. As soon as

I got home from church that night, I was going to eat a container of applesauce.

I wait for my husband as he counsels after each Sunday evening and Wednesday evening service. More often than not, we arrive home past 11:00 p.m. That night I knew it would be a long time before I got to my applesauce, but I looked forward to it nonetheless.

After church, as I sat in my vehicle reading a book, there was a knock on the window. I rolled down the window, and one of the teenage boys in our church handed me a brown bag and said, "Here, my mother wanted me to give this to you." Inside the brown bag were three items: a plastic spoon, a napkin, and a container of applesauce. As you might imagine, I ate the applesauce with great delight. No queen ever enjoyed a feast more than I enjoyed my applesauce from Cindy Mercer. I felt I was eating a love gift from God.

Do you think it was a coincidence? Well, let me ask, "Have you ever received applesauce from a teenage boy?" or "Have you ever thought to yourself, 'I would like to do something for someone. I think I will send that person a container of applesauce.'" God told a Spirit-filled church member what her pastor's wife needed to feel loved. Cindy Mercer was listening, and God showed His love to me through Cindy Mercer and through applesauce! Whatever disappointments and hurts I experienced that day were washed away with a container of applesauce.

2. **Read your Bible and pray daily.** Of course, it is of utmost importance to the person who is hurting (whether it be through the divorce of a mom and dad, the waywardness of a child, the rejection of a sibling, the abandonment of a spouse, or in any other way) that a daily walk with God be priority.

3. **Counsel with one older person.** When you are deeply wounded by a family member, do not go from person to person telling them your problems. Young person, do not go to your

peers. Whether it be a pastor, a pastor's wife, or whoever, find one older godly person whom you trust and use that person for a counselor. Do not be afraid to tell the whole truth. The counselor cannot help you if you do not. But don't betray the truth to more than one person.

Fellow Christians, let's be careful about asking questions and making suggestions to those whom we know to have family problems. In doing so, we may tempt a person to tell us something they did not want to tell and really should not tell.

4. Don't blame yourself. Your parents' divorce is not your fault. Your sexual abuse is not your fault. Your child's failed marriage is not your fault. If we could know whose fault the problem was, it still would not fix the problem. In my experience, most family problems are the result of mistakes made by many people, and no blame can be fairly placed on just one person. Carrying guilt around is to carry the Devil's load and not the Lord's.

This may seem a bit paradoxical, but I have gone to the Lord and asked Him to forgive me for the sins of others. I have asked God to forgive me for the sins of others as well as for any part I might have had in their sins. I frequently ask God to forgive me for the sins of America, but I do not carry guilt around for my sins or the sins of others. I know when I leave the throne of Jesus' mercy, I am thoroughly cleansed, and I do not ask for forgiveness for the same thing over and over. Even the person who has suffered the dirtiest sexual abuse for the longest period of time can be cleansed and be made as innocent as a newborn child.

5. Don't blame God. I believe that one of the greatest themes of my husband's preaching is the sovereignty of God. God made me, and He died an awful death for me. I give God the benefit of the doubt in any question I might have beyond that. God is always holy and just. He loves me supremely. Any sin or hurt is allowed by God but is caused by the world, the Devil, and the flesh. Don't think God is mad at you or punishing you.

6. Don't blame anyone else. As I have already mentioned, most family problems are the fault of many people, humanly speaking. We cannot know whose fault it was that your parents divorced. Children usually want to side with one parent and against the other. There is almost always fault on both sides. Blaming a parent doesn't fix the marriage.

Concerning the matter of sexual abuse, it is the fault of the perpetrator, of course. A wonderful truth that I learned from my father is this: do not see people as good or evil; see them as broken. It is good and wise to avoid the sexual abuser, to recognize him as the one at fault, maybe even to have him put in jail, but it is never good to hate him. The Bible does not give us license to hate anyone.

7. Don't take responsibility to fix the problem. The child should not try to fix his parents' marriage. The parents of the wayward adult child probably cannot fix their child's spiritual problem. The sibling cannot spiritually change the life of a sibling. A friend cannot heal a backslidden friend. I have lived by this policy during my husband's and my ministry: don't give advice unless the person in trouble is asking for it.

One time, after expressing my unconditional love for a wayward friend, I gave that friend some unsolicited advice. I gave the person what I thought was a very loving lecture. In retrospect, I do not think I would do it again. I don't regret doing it because I can't take it back anyway. I just don't think it did any good, and it may have done harm. I wish I would have just given the person my love.

8. Don't socialize much, if at all, with a family member who is backslidden. While each family member needs your love, a time does come when it is no longer wise to "hang around" that person. When you cannot trust the person around your children, when they could bring harm to your spiritual life, your marriage, or your ministry, these are times that family bonding must be kept to a minimum. I'm not talking about avoiding a family member because he (or she) doesn't dot his (or her) *I*'s the way you do. I am talking about limiting especially non-planned time around those who would endanger your other relationships and your relationship with God.

This type of separation is an exception to the rule; but in this wicked world, it does become necessary more often than some might think.

9. **Be an encourager, even in your hurt.** The Bible does tell us in Romans 12:15, *"Rejoice with them that do rejoice, and weep with them that weep."* Often, those who have family problems become obsessed with their own problems. Prayer is the answer to avoiding this. Having a set time each 24-hour period when you thoroughly tell God your hurts and requests regarding your problem and then forgetting about the problem until the same time the next day can help you to be a fruitful and useful Christian, even though your heart is hurting. A statement that has helped me with hurts through the years is this: "You become what you hate!" You also become obsessed with what (who) you hate. This is one reason why I have not allowed myself to hate anyone. I have too frequently seen family problems repeated in the next generation because the person I was counseling obviously hated the mistakes of their parents before them.

10. **Don't take it out on your friends.** Those who have family problems, no matter how severe, do not have a right to make those miserable around them. Family problems may be a reason a person is unkind, but they are not an excuse. Family problems must be dealt with properly, or all those around you will suffer.

11. **Honor your parents.** I know there are some parents who are difficult to honor. On rare occasions, there are those who should even be avoided for safety's sake. Usually, there is a way to honor even those parents who are divorced, abusive, and so forth. One way to honor such parents is not to expose their sins to your

peers. Your parents' mistakes are not an excuse for you to say whatever you want about them to whomever you choose. As I have already suggested, choose one counselor only. Find the good about your wayward loved one and spread it. When nothing good can be said, say nothing. You should only reveal the mistake of a loved one if it is necessary to protect someone else.

Even an abusive parent could be sent a card long distance with a short but sweet message. This should be done not to gain the acceptance of your loved one (this may never happen), but rather to prevent hatred and obsession from becoming a part of your own life. Mainly it should be done in obedience to God.

12. Follow the best Christian. It is especially hard for teenagers to know what to do when their parents divorce. They love both parents, and often one chooses a lifestyle that is very different than the other parent. I like to advise every young person to follow his or her father—Dad should be the king of the home. Unfortunately, at times Dad is the one who is trying to turn his children against what is right. In situations like this, I advise the children to make their individual decisions by following the best Christian.

13. In the area of sexual abuse, I believe the abused should share the truth of her abuse with her fiance once they are engaged. You may feel free to disagree with me, but this is an opinion that I have formed through my counseling.

14. Make a list of the positive things that have or could have happened because of your family problem. Our problems bring us closer to God and better equip us to help others. One victim of sexual abuse shared with me that she believes her abuse as a child caused her to be less promiscuous with the opposite gender during her dating in high school.

15. Have a vision. Proverbs 29:18 says, *"Where there is no vision, the people perish...."* Family hurts may kill our vision for the future. They may cause us to feel unworthy. This is one reason why victims of family hurts perish. They fall apart because their future feels hopeless. How could you use your hurt to help others? Get a vision of doing just that, and spend your life preparing to do something that will help others to avoid the hurts you have experienced.

16. Remember, God loves you! I end this chapter where I started it. You may be a victim of sexual abuse, your parents may be divorced, your children may have broken your heart, but the One Who made them all is crazy about you! Hold your head up high and walk forward into your future with hope and love. You have much to offer to all with whom you come in contact!

Step 8

Learn Mind Control!

Living on the Bright Side

FIRST PETER 3:10, 11 SAYS, *"For he that will love life, and see good days, let him refrain his tongue from evil, and his lips that they speak no guile: Let him eschew evil, and do good; let him seek peace, and ensue it."* I think that everyone would like to wake up each morning and be able to honestly say, "I love life!" We all would also like to go to bed each night saying, "What a great day!" The Bible plainly tells us how we can love life and have good days. The secret is in the tongue. If we do not speak evil, we will love life. How do we refrain from speaking evil?

1. **We should eschew** [totally avoid] **evil** [those sins that hurt people]. A good way to avoid evil might be to avoid being around people who speak and perform evil.

2. **Do good.** I believe the Bible is telling us that we will only DO good if we first SPEAK good things.

3. **Seek peace.** Again, I believe the Bible is teaching us that avoiding the speaking of evil things is an aggressive way to pursue peace.

Four Life-Changing Philosophies

Four life-changing philosophies that can be learned from I Peter 3:10, 11:

1. Negative (evil) thoughts always lead to negative words.
2. Negative words always lead to a negative life. They cause us to hate our life and have bad days.
3. Positive thoughts always lead to positive words.

4. Positive words always lead to a positive life. They cause us to love our lives and have good days.

Crabby old ladies are often ladies who have lived lives that are full of regrets. Their poor thinking and speaking has caused them to make decisions that have caused them to hate the life which they have lived. You don't become a crabby old lady all of a sudden. You are planning today what kind of a lady you will become by the thoughts you choose to think today and the words you choose to say today.

You may say, "I can't control every thought I think and every word I say." To this I answer, "Oh, yes, you can!" I used to think that I had no control over my mind. Since then, I have learned to be in charge each moment of the thoughts that I think. I am not saying that bad thoughts never come into my mind; but if they do, I have learned how to ignore them and how to replace them with positive thoughts. Of course, I am made of flesh; and I am not totally consistent, but I do take RESPONSIBILITY for all of my thoughts. This is the first key to controlling my mind. **If I do not control my mind, it is true that I cannot have control over my tongue or my actions.** Therefore, I lose control of my life.

Allow me to summarize the preceding paragraph. "You can't change your life until you first change your mind." The Devil and God are in a battle for your life. The battlefield on which they wrestle is your mind.

Helps to Live on the Bright Side

Another way of thinking about this, which helps me to live on the bright side, is the following:
1. Sorrow and joy are in a battle for my life.
2. The Devil is on the side of sorrow.
3. God is on the side of joy.
4. The battle between sorrow and joy takes place in my mind.

5. I am on God's side, so I am on the side of joy.
6. I am determined that God and I are going to win! I am going to have joy!

Some Common "Death Thoughts"

In the following paragraphs are listed several common "death thoughts" that we need to avoid in our lives.

Suspicion. Sometimes my woman's intuition has spotted trouble and has been correct. In spite of this, I generally ignore my intuition. This tool is something the Devil can use to cause women to have minds full of suspicion and mistrust. Don't be suspicious of people, even if they have let you down. If all you have is intuition and no facts, I would take your intuition to the Lord in prayer and leave it there.

Evil forebodings. Do you ever wake up and just feel like something bad is about to happen? I do! But I have learned that most often this is just an unfounded feeling the Devil tries to use to give me a bad day. I ignore evil forebodings.

Judgment. This is forming an opinion about another's behavior with limited information. I like to stay out of the "know" about things so that I am not tempted to judge a situation about which I do not have all the facts.

Self-criticism. Thoughts such as "I'm crazy," or "God doesn't love me," or "God doesn't want anyone else to love me" are death thoughts and should be put away quickly.

Criticism. Thinking about what is wrong with others will lead to negative words, negative days, and a negative life. Criticisms are death thoughts.

Worry. Wondering what will happen tomorrow or even later on today leads to death thoughts. Instead, focus on the present moment and trust God with your future and your problems.

Daydreams. Wishing you were someone else or married to

someone else is a dead end; and it causes a person to have bad days and to hate his/her own life. Choose to think about what is reality and do not waste your life fantasizing about something pretend.

Some Great "Life Thoughts"

Instead of allowing these death thoughts to possess your mind, why not replace them with positive thoughts. Let me give you some ideas of some great positive thoughts to cultivate in your mind.

Thoughts about God. My husband is crazy about God. I believe that is the key to his great preaching. He does not have to set aside sermon preparation time to think about God. He is always thinking about God, and it spills out in his sermon preparation and delivery. I am also crazy about God, and I want my mind to reflect how wonderful He is.

Thoughts about God's love. As stated already several times, each day I ask God to show Himself to me. Then I look for Him. I even have specific things I look for and, when I see them, I say to God, "I see You, Jesus. I know You love me, and I love You, too!"

As I have already mentioned, I have been encouraging ladies everywhere I go to keep a journal, writing down each day one thing God did to show them He loves them. I did this one year, beginning on New Year's Day and finishing on Thanksgiving. I sat down on Thanksgiving and read the entire journal. It was amazing what God had done for me.

This thinking has changed my life and made me a very positive person. It has been said that "Revival is a new awareness of God in your life." If so, then I have experienced revival in the past three years. God has seemed so real, and in spite of many struggles, my days have been great and I have loved life.

Thoughts about God's power. We need to mull over in our minds the great things that we see God do each day. For example, last Sunday morning in our church, a man and woman from Russia were saved. We just happened to have a Russian missionary in our service. He and his wife have had a hard time understanding why God has kept them from getting back to the field. But they were needed in our service to win two Russians to Christ. I take an experience like that and repeat it to myself and others over and over. I also remind myself frequently how much God wants to use me.

Thoughts of praise. I praise God over and over for the blessings I see in our services each week, as well as every other day. I think God likes to show off more for those who make a big deal of everything He does. I have seen this at work in my own life.

Thoughts about the Bible. I began memorizing the Bible several years ago, and this has helped my mind and attitude. I also underline verses in my Bible and read them throughout the day. I keep a perpetual calendar of Bible verses on my night stand. I look forward to changing my calendar each morning and seeing my verse for the day. Each time I go near my bed, I stop to read this verse. Sometimes my husband sees me change my calendar and asks me, "What is our verse for today?" My husband and I love to talk about the Bible, and we have a very positive marriage. The Bible has the answer for everything.

Edifying thoughts. We should always be thinking edifying thoughts about other people. It would be a good idea to replace every critical thought about a person with an edifying thought about that same person. Example: "She doesn't dress as modestly as I think she should." Replace with: "She sure is friendly to me when I see her."

Philippians 2:5 says, *"Let this mind be in you, which was also in Christ Jesus."* God never gives us a command that we cannot obey. We can (and do) have the mind of Christ. It is our responsibility to let His mind abide in us. When we do, we bring upon ourselves for His glory many wonderful days and a wonderful, wonderful life.

Having the Mind of Christ

The following are some signs that the mind of Christ abides in your mind.

A Focused Mind. The mind of Christ can focus intently on the present. Some Christians have a mind that is always wandering somewhere else. They cannot focus on preaching or much of anything else. Some people may be diagnosed with ADD (Attention Deficit Disorder), when their real problem may be that they have a mind that has been filled with too much negative.

A Clear Mind. The mind of Christ is clear and can easily make decisions. Some people's minds are so full of negative that they are weakened in their decision-making ability. They have a miserable time just picking out what to wear in the morning.

A Mind of Faith. The mind of Christ is not confused and doubtful. The mind of Christ is not a wondering mind; rather the person lives in and enjoys the present, not wondering what might happen later on today or tomorrow.

A Mind of Rest. The mind of Christ is not overloaded and busy. As Christians, we should be busy serving God but not so busy that we cannot hear God. You cannot hear a quiet voice if you are always in a room full of noise.

How to Obtain the Mind of Christ

To obtain the mind of Christ, I want to share some practical ideas on how to think and speak positively. The mind of Christ is a mind full of positive thoughts.

1. Begin to praise God as soon as you wake up in the morning. It is easy to be negative when you first wake up. This is a bad way to start a good day. When I awaken, I immediately begin to thank God for a new day.

2. Praise God if you wake up during the night. Do you ever wake in the night troubled? I do. Sometimes I think this is more of a physical reflex than it is anything else. If I wake up in the night, I either think positive thoughts or I pray.

3. Be a woman of the Word. The men of this generation need wives who are strong and clear in their thinking. The more you know the Bible, the more you will think like Christ.

4. Take all of your problems to God and leave them there. Each day I take my problems to God. We discuss them thoroughly. Then I trust them to God and don't think about them until the same time the next day.

5. Keep your mind busy. "An idle mind is the Devil's workshop." If your mind is bored, stimulate it with a sermon tape or praise music. Do not allow it to wander.

6. Ignore all negative emotions. My husband and I have both agreed that we feel every possible emotion there is to feel in any given 24-hour day. You cannot carry the responsibility my husband carries without feeling every emotion. What do we do about these emotions? We ignore the bad, and we emphasize every positive emotion that we feel.

7. Do a Bible study on faith. Underline verses containing the words "fear," "afraid," "trust," "faith," "strength," and "courage." Write lessons in your journal of what you can learn from these verses. I have done this without even using a concordance, and it helped so much.

The Bible says that unbelief causes us to miss the rest God has planned for us. I am daily trying to build my faith, and I have been for many years. This has put a smile on my face and made me a much more positive person.

8. Live in reality. Live in the present, and live one day at a time.

9. Look for the best in your present circumstances. During the 2003 Christian Womanhood Spectacular, I stacked a pile of bricks on a table. The pile of bricks represented the stronghold that the Devil once had in my very negative mind. All of the sins with which we struggle are represented by some "stinking thinking." The Devil has a stronghold in our minds, but Jesus is called the "strong hold" in Nahum 1:7. *"The LORD is good, a strong hold in the day of trouble; and he knoweth them that trust in him."* He does have the power to change our mind and to remove strongholds.

All strongholds begin with a lie from the Devil. Some examples of the Devil's lies which may control a woman's mind are:

- "I don't need a man."
- "If I submit to my husband, he will hurt me."
- "My marriage problems are my husband's fault."
- "I can't trust my husband."
- "I can't trust people."

The root of all strongholds is the one lie which was told in the Garden of Eden: "You can't trust God; you can't trust God's Word."

Victory Over Strongholds

Here is the process that I have experienced in gaining victory over the stronghold of "stinking thinking."

1. The Christian begins to seek help from the Word of God. Though I have been in the Bible fairly regularly since the age of eight, I increased my memorization and my study of the Bible about 12 years ago.

2. The stronghold is destroyed slowly and little by little. As I got more and more into the Bible, God sent much success to my spiritual life and in the areas of my marriage, child rearing, and ministry.

3. The Devil sees he is losing his grip, so he adds pressure to the Christian's mind; he adds to the stronghold. I feel that about seven or eight years ago, the Lord allowed me to go through a spiritual valley. I was confronted face to face with God and my stinking thinking. My mind felt imprisoned by thoughts and attitudes that I thought I had already overcome in my life. I learned I had not really overcome them as much as I had just glossed them over. The Lord knew I needed complete victory; it seemed God allowed the Devil to test me sorely.

4. **The Christian may believe the Word of God to be unreliable.** I remember in my own experience being disappointed that God had shaken my lovely, almost fairy-tale existence with my husband and our children. I had served the Lord and built a wonderful life. Couldn't He just work in my life by sending hummingbirds and deer? God knew that He could not use me the way He wanted until my life was changed to be more what would please Him. Before my life could be changed, my mind had to be changed, which is true for every Christian.

5. **The Christian may give up in her mind and seek help from worldly sources such as antidepressants.** I remember sitting on my bed one day and thinking, "If there was a pill to make this all go away, I would use it; but I know God does not want me to."

I am not saying there is never a time to take an antidepressant or another pill to make a Christian's mind feel better. I believe there may be a time when someone with an illness or an injury to the brain should use such a drug. I do believe it is unwise and perhaps unbiblical to use antidepressants to solve our problems in our spirit. Antidepressants should be used as a last resort, if at all, and not as a first response. I believe that sometimes when God is trying to work in the mind or the spirit of a Christian, antidepressants may allow that person to function better, but it never gives God time to do the work that He wanted to do. The Christian simply pops a pill in her mouth and runs along ahead of God.

Also, I believe that antidepressants are unproven. One doctor shared that he only recommends such pills for those whose lives are practically non-functionable anyway. He mentioned great concern about the long-term effects of antidepressants on the minds of those young girls who continue to take them for many years.

From my own counseling, I have learned that antidepressants dull the mind. One girl said, "I never feel sad, Mrs. Schaap, but I never feel happy either. I just don't care. I would like to get off these pills, but I can't." I also have found that the need for such pills increases. One woman I know began taking one pill a day and now takes 15 antidepressants a day.

I do not judge individuals regarding the use of antidepressants. I honestly would rather not even address the issue. Though I am not going to get on a bandwagon about this subject, I do feel that I have the ear of enough people that I have a responsibility to address this issue. My husband and I have discussed the subject thoroughly and are on the same page regarding it.

6. The Christian may instead continue to trust and to seek the Word of God. In spite of a season of depression, I continued to seek the Word of God more diligently than ever and resisted the desire to try some other "fix." It was only by the grace of God, but I cannot tell you how many times I have gone back to that day by my bed and thanked God for the decision I made. If you are going through a time of depression in your life, my advice to you is this: "Hold on my child; joy comes in the morning!" The Word of God does work; it is the answer...for everything!

7. The Almighty God destroys the stronghold. One day God took His strong hand and pushed away all of the bricks of "stinking thinking" that were stacking in my mind. It seemed that I took two steps forward and then one step back; yet, in a way it seems that God did it all at once. I do know that I was once quite a negative person; whereas, I am now consistently thanked for my constant smile by those who know me. I often think to myself, "If they only knew how God put the smile on my face!"

God is the Almighty, and He does have the power to change your life and your mind, all the way from completely negative to completely positive—regardless of your circumstances.

8. Part of the stronghold is left behind to keep the Christian depending on God. I would say that my "stinking thinking" is 95 percent healed. I think I will probably carry with me five percent of wrong thinking from past hurts for the rest of my life. This is the thinking that sends me to my knees every day begging God to help me. Seven years ago, I learned in a new way that I can do nothing without God, and I am so glad I learned this fact!

9. The Christian enters Canaan. Not long after God did so much work on my mind, my father went to Heaven. One month later, my husband became pastor of First Baptist Church of Hammond, Indiana. This is an event that is too big for my husband and me not to talk about, and yet a difficult one for us to mention. It started with the death of my father and the resulting change of title for my mother, from pastor's wife to former pastor's wife. Neither my husband nor I would have chosen for this to happen. But God prepared us for it.

I honestly believe I grieved, or at least I learned how to grieve, my father in 1997—four years before his death. A process that once seemed so unkind for God to put me through now seems wonderfully kind. We have a wonderful and loving Heavenly Father. I guess God did lead Brother Schaap and me into a Canaanland He had prepared for us on March 7, 2001. Our plan is to serve in this Canaan for as long as God will allow us. How we love the green pastures of the First Baptist Church of Hammond, Indiana! But if God were to choose to lead us away, I believe that my mind would still be at rest because Canaan is a condition of the mind. My mind entered Canaan in 1997. Yes, my mind has been tempted to leave. Yes, I have felt many emotions since the death of my father and my husband's election to the pastorate. But I have fixed my mind upon Canaan, and I never want to leave.

Hebrews 4:9 says, *"There remaineth therefore a rest to the people of God."* Hebrews also tells us that Christians do not enter into that rest because of unbelief. The *rest* being address here, I believe, is "peace of mind." When we focus our minds on the positive (the bright side), we can have peace of mind in spite of any emotional or spiritual attack. Though I have felt every emotion one can feel in recent years, I have, at the same time, always felt peace. It is said of wisdom in Proverbs 3:17 that *"...all her paths are peace."* This can be said of my journey since the death of my father on February 6, 2001.

Christian lady, isn't it time that you changed your life? You cannot change your life until God first changes your mind. It is your time to enter into your Canaan, instead of wandering around in the wilderness. Your Canaan can start today, right where you are, but you need to hurry and get there. God has great things He wants to do through your life. My prayer for you, my friend, is that you will live happily ever after while always looking on the bright side!

Focused Attention

$\mathcal{I}$T HAS BEEN COMMON through the years for doctors to encourage their patients to not think about their pain. Parents try to calm apprehensive children who are receiving a shot to "think about something else—something happy." Women in childbirth are encouraged to bring a picture of a pretty scene or a loved one with them to the hospital. Looking at the picture helps them to forget their pain. Fixing or focusing our attention upon something that makes us happy helps us to forget our pain.

God gives a similar remedy in Psalm 57:7, "*My heart is fixed, O God, my heart is fixed: I will sing and give praise.*" To *fix* means "to give complete and steady attention to." We can give our focused attention to many things. We can fix our attention upon our personal problems, bad news, or our fears. But there are two things in the Bible that God tells us to fix our hearts upon.

1. Fix your heart upon praise. "*O God, my heart is fixed; I will sing and give praise, even with my glory.*" (Psalm 108:1) This means that all day every day we are to give steady and complete attention to praising God. I have a long prayer list. I love to go all the way through that prayer list, especially on the days that I am home or in the car a lot. I find that the more I pray, the more I praise God. For one thing, I see more answers to prayer, and I have more for which to thank God.

I also find that singing or listening to praise music keeps my heart fixed upon praising God throughout each day. The Devil tries to put my mind upon fear and anger, but I say to myself, "I'm not going there," and I fix my mind upon praise.

Going outdoors helps me to praise God. Yesterday I took a walk. It is the end of March at this writing, so this was one of my first walks in a while. The weather was only 50 degrees, but it was sunny and seemed very pleasant after a long, cold winter. I noticed myself talking to God more spontaneously than I had in a while. I praised Him for the clear blue sky, the sunshine, the milder weather, the blue jay and the robins I saw. I thanked Him for the killdeer. This is a long, skinny-legged bird with which I became familiar last summer. I silently welcomed back a killdeer as he scampered in front of me on his skinny legs, and I praised God for sending the little bird right in my pathway.

It seems almost impossible to have constant feelings of praise, but I find that I praise God much more than I used to. In my own personal life, prayer, music, and nature have been the primary tools God has used to build my praise life. In fact, one of my main praises to God is this: "Thank You that I can talk to You about everything."

2. Fix your heart upon trust. Psalm 112:7, "*He shall not be afraid of evil tidings: his heart is fixed, trusting in the LORD.*" In spite of the overflowing blessings of being a pastor's wife, I must admit that I am faced each day with many fears, hurts, and problems— just as everyone else in this world is, I suppose. The prayer I most often pray when these negatives come my way is this: "Dear God, Help me to trust You." Sometimes it seems I pray this prayer 100 times a day.

The other day I was reading my Bible, and I came across the following verse: Luke 22:32, "*But I have prayed for thee, that thy faith fail not….*" Jesus was talking to Simon Peter, but the reminder that Jesus prays and intercedes for us was comforting. This truth that Jesus prays for all of us is clearly taught in Romans chapter 8.

The specific prayer was also a comfort to me. The thought— that as I am praying and asking God to help me to trust Him, Jesus is asking God for the same thing—makes me feel more than ever that I truly can trust God. Jesus prayed that Peter's faith would not fail. In other words, He prayed that Peter would stay *fixed* ["steadily attentive to"] his faith.

In the 47 years of my life as a preacher's daughter and as a preacher's wife, I have learned more and more just how trustworthy God is. Any fear, any weakness, any problem can be melted away with the comforting words of "Jesus, I trust You." It takes a lifetime to learn to trust God, but allow me to testify that it is possible to grow more and more focused on trusting God.

In the words of our son Kenny's favorite song:

'Tis so sweet to trust in Jesus,
Just to take Him at His Word;
Just to rest upon His promise,
Just to know, "Thus saith the Lord."

Jesus, Jesus, how I trust Him!
How I've proved Him o'er and o'er!
Jesus, Jesus, precious Jesus,
O, for grace to trust Him more!"

Living Above the Clouds

I THINK OF FEBRUARY AS being a cloudy month—not just a cloudy month, but a soupy month. In Northwest Indiana, the weather in February is not really hot or really cold. I honestly prefer a very cold January day over a February day because on most very cold days the sky is clear and the sun is shining. February is usually around 45° with very low clouds and moisture that just kind of hangs in the air. The low clouds and moisture bring with them a darker atmosphere, even when it is daytime.

I make it a practice when I am driving on a February-type day to sing the words to this familiar hymn:

*T*here's sunshine in my soul today,
More glorious and bright
Than glows in any earthly sky,
For Jesus is my light.

CHORUS:
O there's sunshine, blessed sunshine,
When the peaceful, happy moments roll;
When Jesus shows His smiling face,
There is sunshine in the soul.

My dad, who went to Heaven on February 6, 2001, was often described as living above the clouds. He preached a sermon by the same title. I have learned in my own life that living above the clouds is not "spooky." Rather, it is a choice. In my Bible reading several months ago, I found a prescription I had not found before on living above the clouds. Isaiah 33:15 and 16 says, *"He that walketh righteously, and speaketh uprightly; he that despiseth the gain of oppressions, that shaketh his hands from holding of bribes, that stoppeth his ears from hearing of blood, and shutteth his eyes from seeing evil; He shall dwell on high: his place of defence shall be the munition of rocks: bread shall be given him; his waters shall be sure."*

How do people live on high or above the clouds?

1. They do right.
2. They speak right.
3. They have no part in any dishonest gain.
4. They do not listen to violence.
5. They do not watch evil. (As I have already mentioned, evil is the specific sin of one person hurting another.)

When I see the first step of living above the clouds, I immediately think of the importance of Bible reading and prayer. It is my walk with God which helps me to choose to do right. God works righteousness through me; I cannot work righteousness on my own.

When I read about steps two through five, I immediately think of the importance of avoiding gossip and criticism. I am reminded of the importance of never trying to hurt another person.

However, as I meditated more on these verses, some other thoughts came to me. I thought of the admonition not to hear violence, and my mind wandered to the extreme violence of today's popular videos, television programs, and video games. I thought of many of the local radio and news shows which report violent crimes such as rape while often sharing explicit and unnecessary details.

When I read God's command not to watch evil, I thought of the many afternoon talk shows that depict real-life evil. While trading at a particular business, I saw a television show where a woman and man were arguing before a live audience as to whether or not a child was his. The fists of both this man and woman began to clench and swing, and the audience began to clap and laugh. As I left the place of business, I did two things. I asked God to forgive me for seeing such a horrible thing and to renew my mind. Then I asked God to take care of the poor child whose picture was put up on the television screen as it was made public that his father didn't want him. I believe that it was the clapping and the laughing of the audience that hurt my heart most of all. I felt like I was leaving the Roman coliseum where the heathen gathered to be entertained in the basest of ways.

When I think of the popular court shows, I wonder if watching these could be considered watching evil. I wonder if it pleases, puzzles, or angers the Lord when He sees His people finding their entertainment by watching husbands and wives sue each other in court.

Many a person (yes, even Christians) goes to bed at night living not only under the clouds but heavily depressed and oppressed by them. "I wonder what is wrong with me?" they ask. "Maybe I need an antidepressant or a psychiatrist. Why am I **depressed?**"

I think that a better question might be, "Why am I **oppressed?**"

You may respond, "That stuff doesn't bother me!" I believe that many people are very bothered by what they see on television and don't really know it.

Is your marriage on cloud nine? Are you riding high in your relationship with your children? Do you live your life with abundant joy and peace? If not, you should measure your life, not up against mine or even against this book, but against Isaiah 33:15 and 16.

I must admit that I do not always measure up to the challenge of these verses, but I strive to; and I have noticed that when I do not, I feel oppressed.

My husband said recently in a Sunday night sermon that I live in another world. He mentioned that my Christian life convicts him. I told him afterward that he must be getting old because he is getting things backward. It is his Christian life that convicts me.

Yet I, in a way, do live in another world. I walk through a world that is filled with things that grieve the Holy Spirit of God Who lives within me. Just the driving by of a simple billboard can grieve my spirit and cause a feeling of oppression within me. I have found, however, that much of the evil in this world is optional. It is my choice as to whether or not I see evil. It is my choice as to whether or not I hear evil. To the degree that I choose evil, I am depressed and oppressed in my life, my marriage, and my relationships. To the degree that I choose to walk with my God and to follow His prescriptions, I find that I am truly able to live above the clouds.

I do walk on cloud nine in my marriage. I am still on cloud nine that I get to be the wife of Dr. Jack Schaap and the mother of Jaclynn Weber and Ken Schaap. I am on cloud nine about the daughter-in-law and son-in-law God has given me. I am on cloud nine about the church and ministry God has given to our family. And I won't even begin to tell you how much I am on cloud nine about our granddaughter Lyndsay and our grandson Raymond.

I do live in another world—above the clouds. Any time I want to, I can choose to come down. I pray the Lord will always give each of us the wisdom and the strength to choose to live above the clouds.

I'm a Control Freak!

I DON'T THINK I REALIZED this until I hit my late 30s or early 40s, but I am a control freak. I think I could describe middle age in two words: losing control. Growing older is all about losing control!

What I Cannot Control

There are four things I have learned (oftentimes the hard way) that I CANNOT control.

1. I cannot control my husband. I learned early in our marriage that I should not try to control my husband. In the chapter "Accepting Your Husband" in my first book *A Wife's Purpose*, I give several things a wife should accept (or not control) about her husband. Some examples are how he works, how he schedules his time, and how he handles people.

The fact that I cannot control my husband has been a lesson I have had to relearn several times. When Jack became vice president of Hyles-Anderson College, our tidy, scheduled marriage was disrupted. Just as I thought I was gaining some sense of control of our schedule again, my husband became pastor of First Baptist Church of Hammond.

Though we have adjusted very well, I can say that in those early days it seemed like everything was out of control for a while. I honestly trust my husband more than any other man, but when he became pastor, old questions from our early marriage cropped up again.

- "Will my husband continue to love me as he did before he was pastor?" (I was trying to control his feelings.)
- "Will my husband succeed?" (I was trying to control his work.)
- "Will my husband make the right decision?" and yes, sometimes, I asked, "Will my husband do it like my dad did?" (I was trying to control his actions.)

Several years of pastoring have passed. During those years, I have witnessed my husband's unwavering love for me, his years of successful pastoring, and one wise decision after another. Has that caused me to stop trying to control my husband? No. What has helped me to stop trying to control my husband is this: I heaved a big sigh, realized I never could, and quit trying!

2. I cannot control my children. Ages three through twelve are great years for a controlling mother. The colic and the terrible two's are behind you. If you have disciplined correctly, children are pure joy. You tell them when to eat, what to eat, when to sleep, when to do their homework, and, for a while, even when to go to the bathroom.

Then comes junior high, when your child becomes more independent from you. He may even dare to disagree with you. He will probably get busier and spend less time with you. He'll spend more time with youth workers, teachers, and friends. (He'll spend more and more time with people whom you can't control either!)

This loss of control culminates when you take them to the wedding altar. What is marriage? In many ways, to a parent, it is complete loss of control. I have enjoyed every stage of my children's lives. I can tell you that rearing children can be pure joy all the way up to the age of my oldest—26. Beyond that, I'll have to tell you later. I began to enjoy my teenage children again when I reminded myself that being a parent is about love, training, and discipline, but it is not about control. Being the parent of married children is about love and love alone!

3. I cannot control other people. This is another lesson I have had to relearn since I have become a pastor's wife. My husband is the pastor of a large church with international influence. There is no way that I can please all of the people around the country and the world who watch what we are doing, let alone the thousands of members of our church.

- I cannot control what people say about me.
- I cannot control what people say to me.
- I cannot control the questions people ask me.
- I cannot control how people feel or think about me.

How do I handle this complete loss of control while I am standing in the limelight?

- I realize that a pastor's wife cannot lean too heavily on a desire for approval.
- I seek the approval of my God and my husband.
- I face the fact that people will say and do things that hurt me, and I cannot be afraid or angered by that.

4. I cannot control the future. Questions about the future come to light nearly every day.

- What will the future hold for our country?
- What will the future hold for our church?
- What will the future hold for my husband and children?
- What will the future hold for me?

To a control freak, all of these questions bring not only cause to worry, but also a great feeling of a loss of control. How do I handle this loss of control?

- I live one day at a time, and I enjoy each present day to the fullest.
- I live in hope—expecting the best for the future.
- I live in faith—knowing that God will give what is best in the future, whether or not it seems like the best to me.

What I Can Sometimes Control

Now I want to share two lists—first, a list of things I can **sometimes** control, and secondly, a list of things I can **always** control.

1. I can sometimes control my schedule. Schedule is essential to a control freak. It helps control freaks to live with themselves. Schedule is what has helped my husband and me transition to the role of pastor and pastor's wife of a megachurch. For example, every morning my husband and I meet for a 15-minute conversation. At this writing, it is now summer, and we meet on our porch for 15 minutes. Sometimes I rub his back; sometimes we just sit and talk. It is also in our schedule to eat a quick breakfast together.

Every Wednesday I call my husband on my way to church. Every Thursday I meet my husband for dinner. We ride back to the church together, and I attend choir practice while he works in his office. Then we ride home together.

There are evenings when we have several hours together. But these are examples of small things we have placed in our schedule to keep us close on the busy days when we don't see each other much. Controlling our schedule not only keeps us close, but it also brings some sense of simplicity and order to our very complicated ministry.

However, every pastor's wife knows that her and her husband's schedule cannot always be controlled. We work hard and diligently to follow our schedule and to keep our scheduled time together. But sometimes things happen that cause us to have to change our schedule. We call these happenings things that are "beyond our control" because they are!

Control freaks should spend their energy that they want to use controlling their husband, children, and others and put it instead upon controlling their own discipline and schedule. Still, the control freak must realize that even her own schedule cannot always be controlled.

2. I can sometimes control my money. Brenda Tefft, the wife of our college faculty member Chris Tefft, gave a talk on finances at a ladies' meeting where I was present. She challenged us (and convicted us, I might add) to get control of our spending.

I'm afraid most Americans think being in control of their money means being able to buy anything they want. I disagree. Though I rarely ask God for anything for myself, I find as I get older, I want more and more things. For one thing, it takes more to make me look good. I thought I would reach a spiritual plane where I didn't want things. Instead, I am learning that I must live with my flesh, and my flesh constantly lusts after and desires more things. If one believes that controlling his money means buying anything he wants, one's whole life is eventually going to be out of control.

Controlling your money means you have the self-control before you spend to ask yourself questions such as these:

- Will owning this item hinder other believers or my effectiveness in my ministry?
- Can I pay cash for this item?
- Will purchasing this item hinder my giving to my local church and to missions?
- Will owning this item glorify God?
- What is my reason for buying this item?
- Can I afford this item?

I am not saying one can never buy anything just because she wants it, but habitual spending without purpose means a life is out of control. We ought to get control of our spending...but there are times when we cannot control our spending. A sudden trip to the emergency room, an unexpected surgery, a sudden car breakdown can cause us to have to spend money we had saved for some other purpose.

What I Can Always Control

Thankfully, there are some things we can **always** control.

1. We can always control our spirit. I didn't say these are things that are easy to control, but we can always control them.

- We cannot control our husband, but we can control our responses to him.
- We cannot control our children, but we can control our love for them.
- We cannot control others, but we can control our attitude toward them.
- We cannot control our future, but we can control our faith in God.
- We cannot always control our schedule, but we can control our reaction toward unexpected disruptions.
- We cannot always control our money, but we can control our attitude toward it.

As my husband has taught us at First Baptist Church of Hammond, our spirit is the thoughts we think or the words we speak to ourselves in our minds. We can control what we tell ourselves in our hearts about the things that happen that we do not like and can't control.

It takes a lifetime to teach oneself how to control his own spirit, but it is worth the effort! Every problem is both spiritual and practical. If we do not solve our problems from both angles, the problem will probably go unsolved. The problem of an out-of-control spirit can be solved both spiritually and practically.

Ideas for controlling a spirit are given in my book *A Meek and Quiet Spirit* in the chapter entitled "Distracted—A Lesson from Mary and Martha."

In a nutshell, we control our spirits in a spiritual way by walking with God and by growing in our walk with God. We control our spirits by placing spiritual food in our lives throughout each day, such as sermon tapes and praise music, and by avoiding that which is spiritually damaging, such as wrong television (most television), wrong literature, wrong music, and so forth.

We control our spirits practically by being scheduled and disciplined in our sleeping habits, our eating habits, and in our habits of exercise. We control our spirits by hanging around with positive people—other people who control their spirits.

2. We can always control our tongue. Again, I didn't say it would be easy, but we can do it! I Peter 3:10, *"For he that will love life, and see good days, let him refrain his tongue from evil, and his lips that they speak no guile."*

In my John R. Rice Reference Bible, the word *refrain* is said to mean "control." God says we are to control our tongue from evil. We are to control ourselves from speaking bad about other people. God would not give us a command that we could not follow.

Again, it takes a lifetime to learn to control our tongue. James 3:8 says it is well-nigh impossible. Yet I Peter 3:10 leads me to believe we can control our tongues from evil. I know in my own life that I have not completely learned to control my tongue, but I have come a long way in this area. Practice has not made perfect, but practice has made much, much better!

How to Control the Tongue

We teach ourselves to think right words in our spirit. A controlled spirit will not be critical of other people. A controlled spirit will have a controlled tongue.

Fellow control freaks, why not take all the energy you use trying to control your husband, your adult children, and others, and use it to control your own tongue? Why not take the energy used worrying about the future and use it to control your own spirit? What a lot of control we control freaks would have then!

More importantly, why not fall on your knees seven times a

day and tell Jesus Christ that you want Him to control everything all of the time. Perhaps while reading this chapter, you have realized you are also a control freak. If you are guilty of nagging your husband, arguing with your teenage or adult children, worrying about what other people think of you, or worrying about the future—you probably are a control freak.

One of the meanings of the Bible word "Lord" is "controller."

- Is Jesus the Lord of your husband/marriage?
- Is Jesus the Lord of your children?
- Is Jesus the Lord of your relationships with others?
- Is Jesus the Lord of your life and your future?

Why not heave a big sigh of relief and give up control over those things that you cannot control anyway? Make Jesus the true Controller of your life by giving Him complete control over your husband, your children, your relationships, your future, and your life. Make Jesus truly the Lord of all! Make Jesus the Controller of your schedule, your money, your spirit, your tongue, and your future. Make Jesus the Lord of all!

Watch and Pray

"Praying always with all prayer and supplication in the Spirit, and watching thereunto with all perseverance and supplication for all saints." (Ephesians 6:18)

*I*T IS WONDERFUL TO me how the Bible never grows boring. I don't understand how I can read the same verse year after year and then suddenly find something new and fresh, but I love it. I often wonder why God didn't reveal certain lessons to me beforehand. When I find them, they usually seem very helpful and yet very simple. Such is the case when I last read Ephesians 6:18 in my morning devotions.

Whenever I see the Bible word *watch*, especially in the New Testament, I consider it to be a challenge to pray for the Second Coming of Christ. I strive to ask the Lord to return daily, and though I love my life here, I am ready for His coming.

But a few weeks ago the word *watch* in Ephesians 6:18 took on a new meaning for me. It is plain to see, but I had never noticed it before, that the Bible is commanding us to watch, not for the Lord's return, but for all of our fellow Christians. Allow me to share with you some other lessons I have gathered from this verse.

1. We are to watch out for our fellow Christians. I believe one of the responsibilities of prayer is to observe our fellow Christians. I did not say to *investigate* our fellow Christians, nor did I say to *question* our fellow Christians. The Bible merely commands us to watch. Like a mother hen, I am supposed to watch my fellow church members. I am supposed to watch for who might be sick, who might be hurting, and so forth.

2. **We are to watch with prayer.** In my observance of my fellow Christians, if I see someone who is hurting or sick, I am to accompany my watching with prayer for the apparent need of the hurting.

3. **We are to watch with supplication.** *Supplication*, as I understand it, means "to agree with God in your prayers." In other words, as we are praying for our fellow Christians, we need to be asking God to have His will in their lives.

4. **We are to watch with perseverance.** In other words, once we see a need in our fellow Christian's life, we should pray for that person faithfully for however long it takes, until in our watching we discover that our prayer has been answered.

Practical Ways to Watch and Pray

Allow me to share with you some practical ways that you can replace your questioning with watching and prayers:

1. **Watch for those who are missing church or appear to be struggling spiritually.** I can think of one individual who was absent from church for many months. I never went to the spouse and asked, "Why isn't your spouse in church?" The Bible doesn't command me to question those who appear to be backslidden; it only commands me to watch and to pray for them. The Bible doesn't command me to tell a friend about my concerns for another. It only commands me to watch and pray for them.

I prayed for this individual for many months. I had him on the top of my prayer list. Soon this fellow Christian returned to church sporadically; then I saw the person regularly. Now it is rare not to see this person in church. From my watching, I believe that I see a changed countenance and other changes in this person. I don't stare at this person, nor have I ever told anyone that I prayed for him. But I have watched and prayed for him. Though I watch and pray for him less, he is still on my prayer list. I never see him in church without silently saying, "Thank You, Lord!"

2. **Watch and pray for those who are single.** There are several ladies and some men in our church whom I pray for God to give them spouses. I don't question these people. "Why aren't you married yet?" "Don't you want to get married?" That is none my business. My business is to watch and pray. Many of these people have been crossed off of my prayer list after a wedding took place. Many remain. Whenever I pray for them, I pray with supplication. I remember that God may have a plan for them to stay single, and I remind Him that I want His will to be done.

3. **Watch and pray for those married couples who are childless.** Several couples in our church have been married quite a few years and have no children. I have not gone to these couples and asked, "Why don't you have children?" "Don't you want any children?" "Can't you have children?" I just watch and pray. Several of these names now have the initials "P. T. L." beside them. That means "Praise the Lord." They now have children. Each time I go through my prayer list, I thank God for their child. Others remain childless. Still I pray with perseverance. As long as they are in their childbearing years, they will have at least one person who will pray with them. I am always pleased to be asked to pray for someone like this. If you would like me to pray for you, please write to Christian Womanhood; I would be honored. But you must keep your end of the bargain: let me know if a child comes because I am not going to ask you. My part is to watch and pray.

4. **Watch and pray for those who have physical handicaps and illness.** It is rude to approach people with questions such as, "Have you ever considered having that fixed?" "Do you think you should go to the doctor?" "Do you think you should do this for your child?" "Do you think you should lose weight?" (There are a

few that I pray for to lose weight!) If you are concerned enough about a matter to be tempted to ask about it, that is a sign that you need to put it on your prayer list. But don't ask! Through my counseling, I am often reminded of the hurtful questions that Christians throw out to one another.

5. **Watch and pray for those who have family problems.** It is rude to inquire about a troubled marriage, a troubled teenager, family problems, and so forth. Too often, it is the curious that question rather than the truly caring. The best words that can be spoken to anyone who is hurting are these: "I am praying for you!" Those words spoken by a truly caring person can speak volumes of understanding that go far beyond the voicing of questions and opinions.

Those who watch and pray squelch the temptation to question and investigate. I am by nature a nosy person. I am also a caring and an opinionated person. These qualities combined could make me a terror as a pastor's wife. When I am really concerned about a matter, I talk to God about it. Just a few words spoken to Him can settle my curiosity, calm my opinions, and give action to my frustrated concern. One of my most oft-repeated statements to the Lord is "Thank You that I can talk to You about everything!"

Those who watch and pray have more things about which to rejoice! Sometimes it seems that everywhere I look at the First Baptist Church of Hammond, there are people who are answers to prayer. I find myself silently saying "Praise the Lord" over and over as I pass the people at our church.

Those who watch and pray learn to love others more. Because God has placed more people in my life than most, I feel a responsibility to love more people. When you fight a spiritual battle with others through your prayers, you come to love them deeply. There are people across the country whom I have never met but whom I love dearly because I have prayed for them for years.

As Christians, I ask you to share with me in the ministry of prayer. Let's replace our nosy questions, our unsought opinions, and our hurtful gossip with prayer and "...*watching thereunto with all perseverance and supplication for all saints.*"

The Lord Is My Portion
A Lesson for the Lonely

I WAS RECENTLY READING MY Bible in my morning devotions, and I came across Psalm 142:5 which says, *"I cried unto thee, O LORD: I said, Thou art my refuge and my portion in the land of the living."* Then I found Psalm 16:5, *"The LORD is the portion of mine inheritance and of my cup: thou maintainest my lot."*

Psalm 73:26, *"My flesh and my heart faileth: but God is the strength of my heart, and my portion for ever."*

Psalm 119:57, *"Thou art my portion, O LORD: I have said that I would keep thy words."*

In the margin of my John R. Rice Reference Bible, I saw that the word *portion* means "expected share." God is my expected share. Allow me to share with you some thoughts on how this Bible study has helped me.

1. God is the expected share of the lonely preacher's wife. My husband takes wonderful care of me—in fact, I am spoiled! But there have been times since the death of my father and my husband's becoming a busy pastor that I have felt lonely. How do I handle this? I realize that my portion is God. All I really need to make me happy is God. Any time that I have with my husband is surplus. This attitude helps me not only to be content, but also to be grateful.

If your time and money from your husband is your expected

share, then it may not be enough. You may be tempted to complain that you did not see your husband as much as you did last week, or perhaps because you don't have as much money to spend on your house as you did last year. If God is my expected share, then any time or any money is surplus, and I am grateful for it.

I think it is impossible to stay in the ministry year after year unless you really love God. A preacher's wife not only needs to learn how to walk with God; she needs to learn how to love God. I love God. I don't just love God: I like God! The more time I spend with Him, the more impressed I am with what I see in Him.

I have always enjoyed being alone. Though I love people and spend much time with those I love, I also enjoy being alone with God. I used to be kind of embarrassed for people to know that fact about me—I thought they would think I was strange or didn't love them. Now I understand that God made me this way for a special purpose; as the pastor's wife, I need to enjoy being alone with God.

If your husband is in the ministry and you do not have a consistent walk with God, I plead with you to find someone who can teach you practically how to know God better.

2. God is the expected share of those who fight materialism in their lives. When I was younger, I thought the sin of materialism (or overspending) was for the young. In my own life, I find that the bend toward materialism grows as I get older. The older I get, the more I like nice things. It takes more to make me look nice!

I exhort myself and others to realize that a "Lot's wife" mentality only increases as we get older. It is not wrong to have pretty things, but it is wrong to have spending habits that are not yielded to God. Should it be our expected share to have a bigger bank account than when we were younger—or should God be our expected share?

My husband and I have lived in the same house for 23 years.

I recently asked my husband if he would like to move to a larger house—just so that we could invite more guests over. My husband replied, "No, because I love our house, and if we moved, I would miss it."

I loved his answer! I have always told myself I would move if I ever became tired of our house; I just have never gotten tired of it. I am not saying it is wrong for anyone to upgrade their living standards. But if God is our expected share, we will be grateful wherever we are. God is the very best life has to offer, and He is mine. On top of that, He has given me a house that is beautiful. Can you believe it? Why would I need more?

3. **God is the expected share of the possessive.** I will admit that I am possessive by nature. I love deeply, and I fight the fear of losing those I love. In just a little over a year's time, my father died, my husband became pastor of a megachurch, my firstborn got married, my mother moved 1,000 miles away, and my last child moved into the college dormitories. Sometime during that year I found myself at my own pity party saying, "No one really belongs to me. Life is all about losing everyone you love." Through this time of great adjustment, God has reminded me over and over that Someone indeed does belong to me. That Someone is just the God of the Universe—the Best—the Cream of the Crop. And He is mine—really, really, really mine every second! I now enjoy my time with others more, and more importantly, they enjoy me more because I am content with whatever time they have to offer me, even if it may be just a few moments.

4. **God is the expected share of the empty nest and the empty bed.** Maybe your nest seems empty because your children have grown and moved away. Maybe your bed is empty because you are a widow. Not only are you lonely, but you don't feel needed anymore. You may ask, "Why doesn't God just take me to Heaven? Nobody needs me here anymore." Deuteronomy 32:9, *"For the LORD's portion is his people; Jacob is the lot of his inheritance."*

Not only is God your expected share, but you are God's expected share! You are all God wants! You are all God needs! I don't think God wants the mansions and the golden streets. They are there to entice us to Him. God doesn't need the hummingbirds, the flowers, or the trees. They are there to attract the attention of what He really wants—His portion is His people!

Lonely widow, God left you where you are because He needs you where you are. You are all God wants. You could be happy again if you would make God all that you want. I'm not talking about becoming a hermit; God wants to use you to be there for your loved ones and others when they need you. But what about when they don't need you, or maybe even don't want you? God will then be your portion, and He is enough to make you happy.

I pray every day that my husband will be alive, healthy, and safe. We both have said that we want to die together after our one hundredth birthdays. We love life, and we love each other. But in case this does not happen and the love of my life precedes me in death, I want to be prepared. I want to delight today in the portion of my life—the Lord Jesus Christ Himself. As my friend from Alabama would say, "God makes me hot-diggety-dog happy!"

I am not a widow yet, nor am I the expert on being lonely. But I have spent much time alone with God these 47 years, sometimes because I wanted to—sometimes because I had to. And I can testify through experience that God is truly our portion; God is truly our expected share, and God is truly enough!

Lasting Influence

"Blessed is the man that walketh not in the counsel of the ungodly, nor standeth in the way of sinners, nor sitteth in the seat of the scornful. But his delight is in the law of the LORD; and in his law doth he meditate day and night. And he shall be like a tree planted by the rivers of water, that bringeth forth his fruit in his season; his leaf also shall not wither; and whatsoever he doeth shall prosper. The ungodly are not so: but are like the chaff which the wind driveth away. Therefore the ungodly shall not stand in the judgment, nor sinners in the congregation of the righteous. For the Lord knoweth the way of the righteous: but the way of the ungodly shall perish." (Psalm 1)

I WAS RECENTLY READING PSALM 1 again in my devotions, and my eyes were attracted to the phrase, *"...his leaf also shall not wither...."* In my John R. Rice reference Bible, the word *wither* is interpreted as meaning "fade."

The form of a tree is its trunk. I once heard Mrs. John R. Rice say, "When a tree is stripped of its leaves, you can best see its form." That quote came to mind 17 years ago when our family was being slandered, and it motivated me to stay faithful in spite of my family's public profile. I realized that during the hard times, I had an even better opportunity to glorify the Lord and to honor my parents by allowing others to see the true character of my "trunk." I wanted others to see how straight and tall I would stand in spite of the fact that my good reputation and influence (my leaves) had been stripped from me.

The fruit of a tree can be many things—apples, oranges, flowers, or sap. The fruit of a tree is that life-giving, life-changing substance that a tree provides. The fruit of a Christian is the souls we have won and the lives we have changed through the power of the Holy Spirit.

But what is the leaf of a tree? The leaves of a tree are the showiness of the tree. A tree in the wintertime can possess its own type of beauty against a cold, gray sky, but it cannot compare to the beauty of a tree that is full of healthy green leaves. That type of tree is much more noticed and admired. The leaf of a Christian is that Christian's influence or reputation, that part of our Christian life that causes us to be noticed and attractive to others. The Bible teaches us in Psalm 1 that there is a way that a Christian's influence can never fade away.

Having grown up in such a large church (our church was proclaimed by *Life* magazine as the "world's largest Sunday school" when I was just 12 years old, and I have attended this church for all 47 years of my life), I have seen many Christians come and go. Add to that the fact that our church has a college; I am amazed at the thousands of people who have passed through the hallways of our church and of my life.

I can think of several students at Hyles-Anderson College who made a big splash—some because of talent and others because of spiritual accomplishments. Those students had leaves that were glorious to look at. They had showy leaves that were greatly noticed; yet, they did not continue on to serve the Lord. Their most successful years of influence were in their late teens and early twenties.

Of course, I have known many others who have grown in their spiritual influence as the years pass, and they continue to do so. One of these is the founder of the Christian Womanhood magazine. Even though Marlene Evans was taken to Heaven at a relatively early age of 68, I still frequently hear people mention how they think of something she taught them and how it helped to solve a recent problem. I often ask our managing editor, Jane Grafton, "What would Mrs. Evans do?" I am still learning from her. In fact, I may have learned more from her since her death than I did in her life. Mrs. Evans' influence and reputation—her leaves—are not fading.

Psalm 1 teaches us that if we want lasting influence, we must be careful where we walk, stand, and sit.

1. We should not walk in the counsel of the ungodly. This means we should not take advice from an unsaved person. May I share a principle of mine? I do not read philosophy books written by unsaved people. I may read a book on cooking by an unsaved person, but I would not read a book on marriage, success, child rearing, how to avoid depression, and so forth by any unsaved person. Why? The Bible tells me not to. I will read a book written by a Christian who does not believe every standard that I do (though I am careful), but I will not read a book on philosophy or relationships unless I know the author is saved.

Even if I am at a Christian bookstore, I read the "about the author" to be sure the author is a Christian. Many times the author will be described as a graduate of a secular university with several degrees, as a clinical psychiatrist, but nothing is mentioned to lead me to believe that he is a Christian. I will not read a book by a stranger unless I have some good reason to believe he is a Christian.

I also would not listen to the advice of the latest guest to appear on Oprah, Jerry Springer, etc. if the person is talking about philosophy or relationships. If they are teaching how to organize a house, I might listen. (Actually, I watch neither of these shows.) Unless I have reason to believe the television guest is a Christian, I would not listen to his advice about life.

2. Do not stand in the way of sinners. The reason I do not listen to advice from the unsaved is that their advice makes sense.

The advice of secular humanism makes logical sense to mankind, but it does not usually make sense to God. If I am walking in the counsel of the ungodly, quite soon I will be standing in the way of sinners. I am not supposed to live my life in a way that is disobedient to God's Word—even if it promises to fix my marriage, give me peace of mind, and so forth.

3. Do not sit in the seat of the scornful. Secular humanism teaches a scornful attitude. It teaches us to question our marriage vows and our authorities. It especially teaches us to criticize churches, preachers, and other Christians. Many an influential Christian has had his leaf fade because he started reading books he should not read. Then he followed the advice of those books and began to do things he should not have done. Soon he began to mock and scorn the people who believe what he once believed. These Christians mock Bible-believing preachers and sometimes even God. Some would even claim to be close to God while they do these things. But they have lost their spiritual influence and whatever they do does not prosper.

How to Have Lasting Influence

There is one thing Psalm 1 teaches us that will help us to avoid walking, standing, and sitting in the wrong places. That one thing is the Bible. We are to delight (or find joy) in the Bible, and we are to meditate in it day and night. I have spent much of my life getting to know the Bible. I read it through yearly; I study it frequently. I have memorized much of it.

1. My knowledge of and love for the Bible helps me to avoid walking in the counsel of the ungodly. Though I avoid reading material on secular humanism, it is my knowledge of the Bible that helps me to recognize it. Sometimes a lady will give me a plan to fix (or end) her marriage that makes sense to my human logic. But if her solution goes against the Bible, I must be able to recognize it and point it out as error. From time to time, I find secular humanism even as I read Christian books. It is my knowledge of the Bible that prevents me from taking (or giving) ungodly advice.

2. **My knowledge of and love for the Bible helps me to avoid standing in the way of sinners.** It is not unusual for a new trend to come out in the world that appeals even to Christians, but having a good knowledge of the Bible can help a Christian to recognize a trend that should not be followed.

3. **My knowledge of the Bible keeps me from sitting in the seat of the scornful.** Sometimes a well-meaning Christian will come to me with the latest gossip about a preacher who I believe is saved and serving God. It is my knowledge of the Bible that pricks my conscience and helps me to remember it is always wrong to sit in the seat of the scornful.

What Is the Promise to Those Who Know and Love the Bible?

1. *You will win souls and see lives changed.* "*...that bringeth forth his fruit in his season....*" (Psalm 1:3)

2. *You will prosper at whatever you do.* "*...and whatsoever he doeth shall prosper.*" (Psalm 1:3)

3. *Your influence will not fade away.* "*...his leaf also shall not wither....*" (Psalm 1:3)

The unsaved and their advice will be driven away. So will the lives be of those who listen to and follow their advice. "*The ungodly are not so: but are like the chaff which the wind driveth away.*" (Psalm 1:4)

I want my books and articles to bear influence long after they have been written and read. I want my teachings to be remembered long after they have been spoken.

I want a life to be changed long after I have passed a person's way. I want my influence to pass from my children to their children and to theirs.

I am not worthy for such goals to be fulfilled, but God has promised this to me if I will heed the words of Psalm 1.

As I began to write this chapter, I looked in a file of many thoughts I had written down. I turned to several Bible passages and decided not to use them this month. I felt impressed to use my notes from Psalm 1. I turned to Psalm 1 and found an outline written by my father. Below is that outline in his own handwriting.

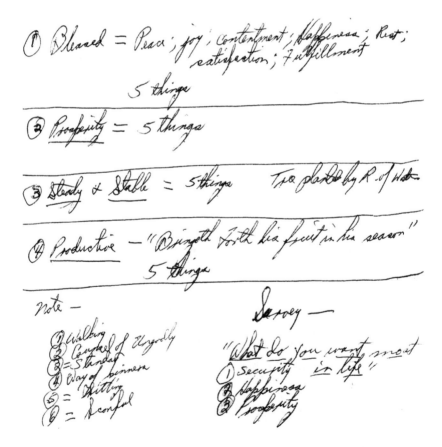

Though my dad has been in Heaven since 2001, hardly a day goes by that I do not think of his teachings. His leaf does not wither. His influence does not fade. It is lasting. May this be true of all of us. All we have to do is follow a simple recipe. We must simply love and think about God's love letter to us—the Bible. *"Wherefore be ye not unwise, but understanding what the will of the Lord is."* (Ephesians 5:17) We must get to know the Bible so that we will have wisdom to understand what is the will of God and what is the will of man.

The Schaap Family

Dr. and Mrs. Jack Schaap are the parents of two children. They have two grandchildren.

Jack Allan Schaap
    October 1, 1957
Cindy Lynn Hyles Schaap
    November 30, 1959

Jaclynn April Schaap Weber
    April 16, 1981
Todd Andrew Weber
    October 21, 1980
        Lyndsay Alana Weber
        March 18, 2005
        Raymond Jack Weber
        August 19, 2006

Kenneth Jack Frasure Schaap
    November 14, 1984
Candace Janel Hooker Schaap
    September 27, 1984

Lyndsay and Raymond